MW00608362

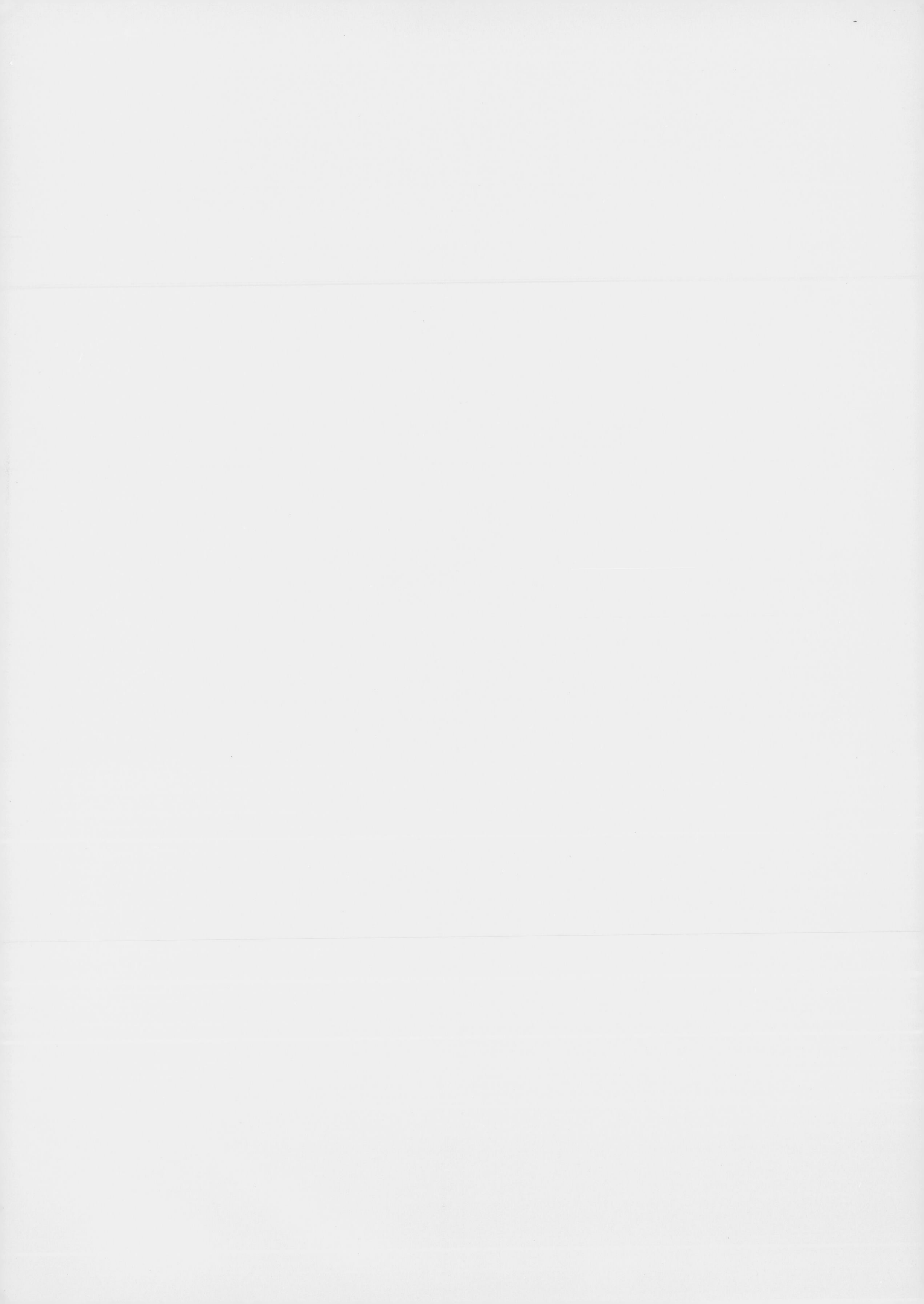

Austin Unlimited

the people, place, passion & prospects

By Kirk Watson with Kate Alexander

Introduction by Dr. Colette Pierce Burnette

J Robert Towery – Publisher

James Tomlinson – Executive Publisher

Ardith Bradshaw – Editor

Linda Wetzel – Assistant to the Publisher

Nikki Sepsas – Profile Writer

Noah Towery – Associate Publisher & Designer

Jacques Verhaak – President & CFO

Published by CityInk Company

www.cityink.com

AUSTIN

UNLIMITED

◄ Music under the live oaks is what it is.

Photos by Noah Towery

▼ Never a dull day inside the Carousel Lounge

Photo by Ed Malcik

▲ Photo by Casey Chapman Ross

Library of Congress Control Number: 2019952330

ISBN-13: 978-0-9741374-3-8

Kirk P Watson, 1958-
with Kate Alexander, 1973-

The tenth volume in CityInk's Urban Renaissance Books series, ***Austin Unlimited*** recounts the city's explosive growth in recent decades. Told by former Austin mayor and state senator Kirk Watson, this account explores the rise of a sleepy 19th century capital into a booming hub of technological innovation and urban growth.

What is the secret to Austin's success? How has it dealt with the pitfalls of growth? Watson's recollections are illustrated with copius color images. That history is enriched with profiles of businesses and institutions that sustain the economy, life-style, health, and education of this thriving community.

Cover photo by Noah Towery

published by cityink company
www.cityink.com
Memphis, TN 901-483-2001

URBANRenaissanceBOOKS a series created by cityink

Printed in Korea

Contents

Preface: Portrait of Dr. Clay Johnston

Dean of the Dell Medical School at The University of Texas at Austin

◀ Clay Johnston has served as the inaugural dean of Dell Medical School and as Vice President for Medical Affairs at The University of Texas at Austin since 2014.

Photo by Kelly West

◀◀ The Dell Medical School

Photo by Albert Vecerka, courtesy of Page

For Dr. Clay Johnston, it was the opportunity to build a medical school from scratch — to rethink everything — that drew him to the brand new Dell Medical School at The University of Texas at Austin.

"I was frustrated with how we did business and how we were organized and how difficult it was to innovate in existing academic medical centers," Dean Johnston said. "This really was an opportunity to ask questions...How could we do it better? How could we accelerate innovations to improve health? And how could we be better aligned with society's interests?"

Dell Med was the first new medical school to be built at a Tier 1 research university in about half a century so there wasn't a clear blueprint to follow. It was a dream job for just about every world-class MD/PhD out there.

During the hiring process, I worried a lot that we'd end up with a preeminent academic with extraordinary credentials but little understanding of the unique, community-focused mission of this medical school.

Fortunately, we got both in Clay. Dean Johnston is certainly a world-class MD/PhD, but he absolutely gets that community is a part of the DNA of Dell Med.

A neurologist who specializes in stroke care and research, Dean Johnston came to Austin from the University of California San Francisco where he led the Clinical and Transitional Science Institute. He had also launched the Center for Healthcare Value at UCSF, which focused on improving care while reducing costs.

His mission at Dell Med is nothing short of creating an entirely new model of academic medicine to drive innovation, improve health and do it all more efficiently.

Dean Johnston has surrounded himself with other visionaries to help achieve that daunting task. It's inspiring to see the quality of the faculty and staff that has been assembled.

They're "Rethinking Everything", as they like to say. And they're doing it by embedding themselves deeply in our community. Tying themselves to our people. All of our people. That's a wonderful return we get for doing this whole medical school thing differently.

A Different Kind of Place

Something has made Austin distinctly different from other places.

To some folks, that something is the beautiful, unique environment that features green rolling hills, craggy limestone cliffs, tree-lined creeks, natural springs and a delicate aquifer below.

To others, it's the quirky, accepting, laid-back atmosphere that has attracted people who want to be true to themselves and think differently. They've brought along their ideas and a passion to create music or a movie or an app or a new way to keep people healthy.

To me, it's all of those things because they captivate the people who are our community, whether they're natives or transplants. Those people make it a special place. They're people who care enough to make some noise when they need to. They love to have a good time. They bring our neighborhoods to life with creativity, personality and humanity.

And they're willing to invest in the future, in their children, in their environment and in their neighbors.

In 2012, they did something that baffles folks who don't know Austin. The people voted to increase their property taxes to create and support a long-desired medical school at The University of Texas at Austin. They embraced our vision in which the medical school would be the catalyst to transform our community's health as well as our economy.

The Dell Medical School at The University of Texas at Austin is unlike any of its peers around the country because the local community is part of its DNA. Dell Med's mission includes a focus on the health and healthcare issues that affect traditionally underserved populations as well as fostering solutions that are available to everyone, regardless of their ability to pay.

Already, the results have been astounding. The year-long wait to see a specialist in joint pain has been eliminated. The rate of screenings for colorectal cancer, which is the second-leading cause of cancer death in the United States, has doubled due to an innovative outreach effort. And new protocols for pain medication have reduced opioid prescriptions for new moms by 40 percent.

Dell Med is also the key to opening Austin to a growing segment of the economy that is driven by the creativity and innovation.

Only a year after Dell Med welcomed its first class of students in 2016, biopharmaceutical powerhouse Merck & Co. Inc. announced it would come to Austin and initally take up residence within the Dell Med's Health Discovery Building.

"We're coming to Austin because it's such a creative, collaborative community, with a strong technology base. Alongside partners like Dell Med and local startups, we hope to combine that with innovation in health care to help improve lives," said Clark Golestani, who was president of Emerging Businesses and Global CIO at Merck at the time of the announcement.

Merck saw something special and distinctly different in Austin and wanted to be in the middle of it. As we grapple with extraordinary growth and change, maintaining and preserving that something will take all of us working together for our community.

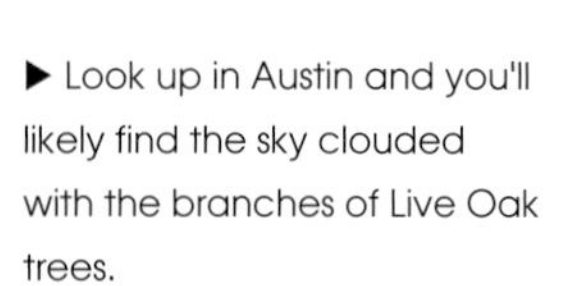

▶ Look up in Austin and you'll likely find the sky clouded with the branches of Live Oak trees.

Photo by Noah Towery.

English
Classes
Register
Now
476-1933
As

Introduction by Dr. Colette Pierce Burnette
Huston-Tillotson University, President and CEO

▲ Dr. Colette Pierce Burnette has led Huston-Tillotson University, the oldest university in Austin, since 2015.
Photo courtesy of Huston-Tillotson Universit

◀◀ Vibrant mural art in East Austin.
photo by Noah Towery

As a newcomer to Austin in 2015, I came to find that the "Keep Austin Weird" bumper-sticker slogan didn't really capture the vibe nor the experience I was having living, playing, and working in Austin. It wasn't weird at all.

It was magical.

And I do believe that if we all work deliberately, we can "Keep Austin Magical."

There is a magic in the creativity, energy and boundless opportunities of Austin's innovation economy, and Huston-Tillotson University — a small, liberal arts minority-serving institution — is immersed in it. We've partnered with tech giants, created a student-run hackathon for high schoolers, launched the hashtag #IAmThePipeline and hosted some very cool SXSW events. Today, I'm proud to say that we're educating the #GeniusGeneration.

One crucial element of any prosperous city is a sense of culture and community. It is what Dr. Martin Luther King, Jr. called the 'beloved community'.

As the city's only historically black institution and the intellectual heartbeat of East Austin, our greatest challenge is ensuring that everyone in Austin can experience the magic. I believe Austin can use its same spirit of creativity, innovation, and energy to ensure inclusive prosperity, and Huston-Tillotson University is pivotal to making it happen – becoming the beloved community with boundless opportunities for all.

Resilience & Grit

Sitting atop Bluebonnet Hill overlooking downtown, Huston-Tillotson University is a hidden jewel in Austin.

Founded only a decade after the end of slavery in Texas, the school is the oldest institution of higher education in Austin and was created to serve former slaves and their direct descendants. We have a long history of resilience and grit. We work tirelessly to provide access to students with limited resources and give them the excellent collegiate experience they deserve.

As a small, private liberal arts university, we offer an intimate education that produces well-rounded, creative thinkers. Our students are smart and hungry for opportunities. They bring a beautiful diversity of ideas and experiences to the workplace. Our students do not need to be saved. They simply need excellent faculty and staff committed to their success and opportunities. That happens on our campus.

And I've made it my mission to show tech firms in Austin and beyond that our students are exactly who they should be looking to hire because they embody the scrappy, focused, start-up mentality to keep going until you get it.

A few years ago, I sat on a panel about the lack of diversity in technology, which is pretty much the same conversation we've been having since I graduated from engineering school about 40 years ago. One of my fellow panelists, a senior-level human resources professional at a local tech firm, explained how difficult and complicated it was to find people of color to fill available positions.

I asked the audience a question: What if Austin had a historically black college right in the center of the city producing over 200 graduates a year?

It got super quiet in the room and the moderator quickly wrapped up the event. But as I made a beeline out the door, a reporter with the *Austin American-Statesman* caught up with me and wanted to talk a bit more.

My message was that tech firms can't simply keep saying they're trying to find people of color to hire. I tell my students to take the word try out of their vocabulary because you're either doing it or you're not. The same is true for tech companies. They're either intentional about hiring people of color or they're not. They must work hard at it. Declarations that qualified candidates of color are hard to find are smoke screens.

For example, every employer wants to hire someone with experience through internship opportunities. Students who have to work to pay for college and sustain themselves cannot afford to take an unpaid internship while students from families with means can. This is a systemic challenge that can be addressed by offering only paid internships. For my students, that can be the difference between preparedness and the ability to step into an opportunity as opposed to not being as competitive through no fault of their own and having to step away.

There is great merit and more opportunity for success with preparedness. Our Career Pathways Initiative starts working with first-year students during the summer before their freshman year to get students oriented to their career of choice and the associated soft skills required. Our objective is to connect these students early to the world that exists outside of the university so they know what they're working toward and will stay steadfast to completion. We rely heavily on mentors and business partners to help our students see the connection between their college studies and their life after college.

Another opportunity for employers is to create an environment of support for all. Create an environment where all creative thinkers are able to put their minds to work and not be dismissed for being different.

Huston-Tillotson University has been resilient in our pursuit of forming partnerships and building strong collaborations and partnerships with non-profits, school districts, and corporations. We believe strongly in the African Proverb 'You can go fast alone, but you go farther together.'

In my role as president, over the years I've sat down with several potential employers, c-suite executives, and community leaders to talk about the university and our students. Many of them listen politely, nod their heads, shake my hand — and then check the box for "minority outreach." Done.

It was quite different when my team of faculty members and staff met with the

▶ The Cathedral of Junk in South Austin embodies the "Keep Austin Weird" motto.

Photo by Erich Schlegel

▶▶ Crowds flock to the Ann Richards Congress Avenue Bridge to watch the enormous colony of bats emerge from beneath the bridge.

Photo by Noah Towery

MEJOREMOS LA
CIUDAD DE AUSTIN
JUNTOS.
austin 3·1·1
austin311.org
LINE

people from Merck. They sincerely wanted to partner with the University and were extremely committed to investing in our students to fill the pipeline.

At first, it didn't seem like a perfect fit. We have computer science and biology, but we don't have bioinfomatics, which is the skill set Merck needed. After brainstorming what a partnership could look like, we decided to be innovative and rethink curriculum, opportunities for undergraduate research, investments into labs, faculty, and infrastructure. What started as an intentional effort to collaborate has turned into a reciprocal and beneficial partnership for all.

This is just one example of how an intentional and deliberative partnership between a small private liberal arts college and a corporate conglomerate can dismantle the myth that it is too hard to diversify and be inclusive.

In Union We Find Our Strength

Merck wouldn't be here but for the Dell Medical School at the University of Texas. And Dell Med wouldn't be here but for the voters of Travis County, who agreed to raise their property taxes to invest in a medical school and a vision for a healthy community.

The healthcare innovation economy that has grown out of that investment has created enormous opportunities as well as responsibilities for the institutions and businesses that are reaping the benefits as part of an ecosystem. For reality to match the story that Austin tells about itself, we must commit to ensuring that the benefits — the magic — reach every single corner of our community.

The Sandra Joy Anderson Community Health and Wellness Center is a promising start. It opened at Huston-Tillotson University in 2016 with the aim of addressing the health needs of our school community as well as the broader East Austin community. This is an on-campus federal-qualified health center — the only one of its kind in the nation on the campus of a Historically Black College and University — in programmatic partnership with Dell Med and Central Health.

▲ The Zilker Holiday Tree, which is strung from a 19th century moonlight tower, shines as bright as the Austin skyline. Twirling under the lights of the tree is a rite of passage for young Austinites.

Photo by Sean Mathis

Huston-Tillotson's student body, faculty and staff reflect the same community need for services, such as healthcare access and education, recreation, and community gatherings. The minority, low-income, uninsured population in East Austin is at high risk for a multitude of chronic diseases, including diabetes, heart diseases, asthma, tobacco-related diseases, arthritis and HIV/AIDS. To launch the clinic, alumna Ada Cecilia Anderson provided a $3 million grant in the name of her daughter, the largest donation in our history.

We are partnering with Dell Med and other community healthcare providers to focus on health disparities in Austin and foster the training of African American doctors and other healthcare professionals. It is my hope that this clinic is just the beginning of something great for East Austin that capitalizes on all the healthcare innovation for the benefit of the low-income communities of color.

The University is also actively involved and aligned with several organizations committed to building a beloved community. We are proud of our collaborations with the Greater Austin Black and Hispanic Chambers respectively dedicated to economic empowerment. We are entwined with the work of Six Square, which is dedicated to improving the quality of life for African American residents through the preservation of history, culture and art. The name refers back to the city's segregationist 1928 Master Plan that forced Black residents to live within a six square-mile area of East Austin and the resulting "Negro District" where African Americans built businesses, schools, churches and a rich culture of community – ZIP code 78702.

Since the late 1800s, Huston-Tillotson has served as an anchor of that District. We are writing chapters in a new history now. The University is an honest broker in that work and committed for another 143 years of resilience and grit – In Union We Find Our Strength.

I am encouraged by what I see happening in Austin. I see a movement unfolding with everyday citizens having courageous conversations and sincerely seeking to do what is right and good for all. I see a commitment to Keep Austin Magical.

Chapter I: The Capital City

The cool water of Barton Springs offered Austinites some respite from the heat in 1930 and today.

Boone Photo Company. [Swimmers at Barton Springs], photograph, 1930-; (https://texashistory.unt.edu/ark:/67531/metapth123874/: accessed August 8, 2019), University of North Texas Libraries, The Portal to Texas History, https://texashistory.unt.edu; crediting Austin History Center, Austin Public Library.

◄◄ Texas State Capitol building

Photo by Noah Towery.

EVEN BEFORE AUSTIN WAS AUSTIN, ITS RESIDENTS WORRIED ABOUT THE IMPACT OF GROWTH AND HOW WE COULD KEEP OUR HOME SPECIAL. AS THEY SAY, THE MORE THINGS CHANGE THE MORE THEY STAY THE SAME.

William Barton, the "Daniel Boone of Texas," settled in 1837 near what would soon be the tiny frontier town of Waterloo. His land featured several natural springs, which he named after his daughters. Today, we know them all as Barton Springs.

Barton had moved up the Colorado River about 45 miles to get away from his neighbors and found a nice, secluded spot. He reportedly lamented to some visitors that he couldn't "bear the idea of being intruded on by settlers," as recalled in "Seat of Empire: The Embattled Birth of Austin."

But they came anyway, thanks to Mirabeau Lamar, who would become president of the fledgling Republic of Texas soon after his visit to Waterloo in 1838.

The area's natural beauty had caught Lamar's eye during a campaign swing/hunting excursion. And Waterloo's location on the edge of the frontier satisfied his yearning for westward expansion.

A congressional commission set out from the city of Houston in 1839 to choose the permanent seat of government, which would bear the name of the "Father of Texas," Stephen F. Austin. President Lamar instructed the commissioners to visit little Waterloo.

They put Austin on the map — literally.

Tasked by Lamar to build a capital city in time for Congress to convene in late 1839, Edwin Waller laid out the City of Austin – what's still our downtown – on 640 acres between two creeks that flowed into the Colorado River. The grand Congress Avenue stretched from the Colorado River (now known as Lady Bird Lake) north up a gentle slope to "Capitol Square."

From its earliest days, there was no guarantee that Austin would survive, much less thrive.

Lamar's predecessor as president, Sam Houston, had deemed the location "the most unfortunate site upon earth for the Seat of Government." And when he returned for a second term as president in

1841, he moved almost all the trappings of government east to Washington-on-the-Brazos.

Austinites, however, held firm to the last remaining official piece of the Republic of Texas: The General Land Office archives.

When President Houston sent a contingent to capture the archives and take them away from Austin, innkeeper Angelina Eberly earned her spot in history by firing off a cannon to save the archives and Austin. We've honored her with a statue on Congress Avenue that the *Austin Chronicle*, the alternative weekly newspaper, deemed the "Best Commission of a Heaving-Bosom."

Eventually, the voters of the State of Texas declared Austin the capital, a decision that was codified in the Texas Constitution of 1876.

Voters also made Austin home to the University of Texas, providing the twin pillars of Austin's economy for a century to come — government and higher education. But they elected to send the university's medical branch to the port city of Galveston, which was a center of trade at the time. It would take more than 130 years before UT Austin would secure a medical school as part of the flagship campus.

Flash Flood Alley

Once firmly ensconced as the capital city, Austin still faced a major existential threat: the Colorado River.

The Colorado River was unpredictable. During a drought, it could be reduced to a trickle. At other times, the Colorado was prone to devastating and deadly flooding.

The City of Austin set out to build a dam to control the river in 1889 and paid for it with $1.4 million in voter-approved bonds. The aim was to tame the Colorado and generate electricity, creating the foundation for industry when the dam was completed in 1893.

But the Colorado didn't cooperate. In 1900, a massive flood destroyed the dam, leaving scores of people dead and a city drowning in debt, washing away Austin's big industrial ambitions.

It took some time before Austin was willing to once again invest in its infrastructure. Mayor A.P. Wooldridge, elected in 1909, focused on laying the essential groundwork for a thriving city. He created a parks system, acquired Barton Springs, paved roads and built a wastewater system.

"A.P. Wooldridge stayed 10 years and he did probably more in those 10 years...that makes Austin what it is today maybe than any other human being that's ever walked Austin," said Lee Cooke, who served as Austin mayor from 1988 to 1991. "He laid so many foundations that all of the rest of us that came after him just built on that."

It wasn't until the late 1930s that the federal government – and a young congressman named Lyndon B. Johnson – helped build the dams and infrastructure that kept Austin from washing away. In turn, the dams created beautiful lakes – known as the Highland Lakes – and a source of hydroelectric power that electrified the Hill Country west of Austin.

Those investments not only stabilized the water but the economy as well, making Austin a pleasant college town anchored by state government and a growing university.

Despite early efforts, Austin never established a robust manufacturing industry, which meant there was little entrenched local interest in protecting the old economy when the new economy emerged on the horizon.

▶ The Colorado River floods Congress Avenue in 1935, just down the street from the Texas Capitol.

[Colorado River Flood], photograph, June 15, 1935; (https://texashistory.unt.edu/ark:/67531/metapth124019/: accessed August 8, 2019), University of North Texas Libraries, The Portal to Texas History, https://texashistory.unt.edu; crediting Austin History Center, Austin Public Library.

▶▶ Paddleboarders near Barton Springs.

Photo by Noah Towery

◀ Kirk Watson

Photo by Doug Beal

◀◀ Reflections of Downtown Austin

Photo by Ed Malcik

THE OLD ECONOMY WAS STILL MOVING ALONG — SOME TODAY MIGHT SAY PUTTERING — WHEN I ARRIVED IN AUSTIN IN 1981.

Fresh out of Baylor Law School, I came to Austin for a one-year clerkship with a federal judge. My wife, Liz, was a reporter and anchor at a local television station. Our plan was to stay for the year and then head back to North Texas because that's where we grew up and we could be near family.

But then Austin sort of wrapped itself around us. And here we are almost 40 years later.

When we first arrived, we were struck by how people making casual conversation would ask where we were from, hear our plan, and then, it seemed like every single time, they'd say, "Oh, you'll never want to leave." That was a common feeling of the time, and one that certainly applied to us — once you experienced Austin, you found a way to stay.

We'd missed the heyday of the Armadillo World Headquarters, Eddie Wilson's music venue that helped Austin become the self-proclaimed Live Music Capital of the World. But there was a lot of live music around town, and we'd hit up the clubs on many Friday nights and then again on Saturday nights after Liz finished the 10 p.m. broadcast. One of my favorite haunts was a tiny place called Snavely's down on Sixth Street, which is where I first heard Nanci Griffith and folks like that. But we could also be found at Antone's, Liberty Lunch and other joints around town, soaking in the music.

More than a few folks in those bands, waiting tables, tending bar or otherwise participating in Austin's life were UT grads who just loved the town and stuck around despite the lack of higher-paying jobs they could find elsewhere. They enjoyed the natural beauty of the place and the easy, cheap, casual lifestyle. Some of those who stayed had interesting — what you might call "weird"— ideas, such as a grocery store that sold stuff like bean sprouts and granola called Whole Foods Market.

So we had an ample supply of smart, creative, multi-talented, underemployed people when the new economy came knocking.

Planting the Seeds

In 1983, Microelectronics and Computer Technology Corporation (MCC) needed a home.

The for-profit research and development consortium had been created by a group of technology companies in 1982 after the Japanese government announced an effort to develop the next generation of computing. Concerned that the U.S. would be lapped by Japan, the competing companies pooled resources to advance basic research.

The consortium tapped retired Admiral Bobby Ray Inman, the former director of the National Security Agency and former Deputy Director of the Central Intelligence Agency, to lead the effort. Inman had been entertaining a lot of offers from major corporations, including Apple and American Express, after he retired from the Navy in 1982, but he settled on the MCC job because it was something "that had never been done before."

First on his to-do list: launch a fast-paced, public site-selection process for MCC's headquarters. Fifty-seven cities in 27 states jumped at the opportunity. Austin, Atlanta, San Diego and Raleigh-Durham made it to the final round.

"In 1983, the national competition for MCC's headquarters motivated city and state governments to realize that the process of regional economic development had changed from one of 'chasing smokestacks' to one of creating conditions for high-tech entrepreneurship," according to the book *R&D Collaboration on Trial*, which chronicles the MCC story.

The economic development assets for cities were changing. The assets of the future were creativity, innovation, imagination. In other words, people and their minds. Places with an educated workforce and the ability to attract and retain those educated, creative people were ripe to lead in the future.

And a lot of those highly-sought-after people enjoy a beautiful place that's open to new thinking. The bumper stickers and t-shirts declaring "Keep Austin Weird" wouldn't show up until much later, but Austin embraced, or at least allowed, new and different thoughts, ideas and approaches.

At the time MCC was looking, Austin had a smattering of high-tech companies in town, including Tracor, a defense electronics company that had been established in 1955 and became Austin's first Fortune 500 company. National Instruments and Radian Corporation had both been created by Austin-based researchers. IBM, Texas Instruments, Motorola and others also had a presence in the city and a UT student named Michael Dell would soon be building computers in his dorm room. But Austin wasn't considered a high-tech hot spot, yet.

For Texas, MCC represented an opportunity to begin diversifying a state economy that was heavily dependent upon agriculture and oil and gas. When Austin made the cut as a finalist, Governor Mark White corralled business and education leaders from all over the state to craft an offer that would lure MCC to Texas. White named one of his top aides, a lawyer and former state representative, Pike Powers, to spearhead the project.

MCC was looking for a locale that offered more than just the traditional business-friendly qualities, such as low taxes and operating costs, according to David Gibson, the associate director of the IC² Institute at The University of Texas at Austin who wrote the book on MCC. Inman stressed that MCC also needed

City Hall

Photo by Kelly West

access to a strong research university with top-flight graduate programs in computer science and electrical engineering as well as a quality of life that would enable MCC to recruit research talent.

That focus on higher education and quality of life "was a switching point for city leaders, chambers of commerce, all those trying to recruit companies in the research-driven innovation economy," Gibson said.

Texas' large incentive package to MCC beefed up higher education by endowing academic positions in computer science and electrical engineering at the University of Texas and increased research support for graduate students in those fields. It also provided a new building for MCC on UT land in North Austin.

Austin won. And folks around the country took notice.

While the impact of MCC on the research landscape is a point of debate, there's little question that it's had a lasting effect on Austin and Texas. The very public MCC search process elevated Austin in the eyes of high-tech executives who were looking for a place to expand.

"Austin's reputation continued to grow as a place to do business, but also as place with a lot of bright people who thought strategically," Inman said.

Locally Grown

Elsewhere on the University of Texas campus, Michael Dell was hatching his own big idea. As a freshman, he developed his model for selling computers directly to the customer and launched Dell Computer Corporation in 1984 with $1,000 in capital.

When Dell was ready to take his company public in 1988, he reached out to two experienced technology leaders in town to serve on the Board of Directors: Bobby Inman and Dr. George Kozmetsky, the founder of the IC² Institute at The University of Texas at Austin and many say the father of our local tech industry.

"George got behind Dell in a big way," said Gibson, adding that they had a direct phone line where Dell could call Kozmetsky at any time.

Kozmetsky nurtured a number of Austin-born companies in addition to Dell, including Whole Foods and National Instruments, because he believed that building up homegrown companies, rather than importing them, was key to building up a regional economy as well as local philanthropy.

"Dell has been an anchor, a keystone company for Austin's emergence as a technology center," Gibson said.

Growing the Ecosystem

Austin's fledgling innovation economy was still tiny when the broader state economy took a nosedive in the mid-1980s. Oil prices cratered, real estate crashed, and banks crumbled. The economic forces at work were much bigger than Austin, and just about every developer and bank in town got pulled down with everyone else.

"It was horrific," said Lee Cooke, who was elected Austin's mayor during the economic fallout in 1988.

But even amid the city's economic turmoil, new opportunity was taking root.

In 1988, Austin won another high-profile, national site-selection competition. This time, it was for the headquarters

▼ New construction by day and by night along South Congress

Photo by Noah Towery

of SEMATECH, a public-private consortium focused on semiconductor manufacturing.

SEMATECH led to Applied Materials coming to town in 1990. Samsung broke ground in 1996 on its first semiconductor fabrication plant in Austin, complete with a Texas-style rodeo, and has now invested more than $16 billion in its Austin facility. AMD, Tokyo Electron, Google, Facebook, Oracle, Amazon and so many more have also established a footprint in Austin.

Apple, which has been here since 1992, has made Austin a major corporate hub in recent years, including a 1.1 million square-foot campus in North Austin that opened in 2016 and some 6,200 employees. Two years later, Apple announced an expansion plan that is expected to make the company the largest private employer in Austin.

And now the United States Army.

In July 2018, the Army made a huge splash when it announced that Austin would become the headquarters of the Army Futures Command.

The sweeping modernization effort, which is the most significant Army reorganization since 1973, required proximity to a talented workforce, top-tier academic programs in science and engineering, private-sector innovation and a good quality of life.

"We do not have time to build this ecosystem. It needed to be ready immediately," Army Under Secretary Ryan McCarthy said at a news conference.

McCarthy added that the success of the Futures Command requires the Army to be in the middle of where collaboration and innovation are happening every day.

"The military, you could argue, is one of the more formal bureaucratic, buttoned-down organizations and they wanted to come to this creative hub," Gibson said. "Keep Austin Weird and all, that's what the military wanted."

▶ Innkeeper Angelina Eberly helped save Austin as Texas' capital.

Photo by Ed Malcik

TAXI
ZONE
TAXI
ZONE

Austin Portrait: Admiral Bobby Ray Inman

Photo by Laura Skelding

The legend of Admiral Bobby Ray Inman often starts with his remarkable mind.

As a young officer in the Navy in 1958, Inman helped avert a military conflict with China thanks to a nearly photographic memory that enabled him to recall hundreds of dispatches and correct bad information that had been passed to the Chief of Naval Operations. He quickly rose through the ranks, becoming the first intelligence specialist to attain the rank of four-star admiral. Inman went on to serve as Director of the National Security Agency and Deputy Director of the Central Intelligence Agency until retiring from government service in 1982.

"He is simply one of the smartest people ever to come out of Washington or anywhere, who dazzles just about everybody he meets," ***Fortune Magazine*** wrote in 1986 as Inman was leaving Microelectronics and Computer Technology Corporation (MCC) to begin his next venture, Westmark Systems Inc.

Now in his late-80s, as Inman tells the story of MCC, he acknowledges the ease with which he can rattle off the exact dates of events from 35 years ago.

"Numbers, dates, safe combinations," Inman said. "Names...names are hard."

Inman remained heavily involved in the tech industry after leaving MCC, including as an early investor in tech giants Dell Technologies and Oracle.

He continues to work as a professor at UT's Lyndon B. Johnson School of Public Affairs, where he began teaching as an adjunct professor in 1987, with courses in public policy and international affairs.

Higher education has remained a top priority for Inman, who serves on the Board of Trustees for the California Institute of Technology.

The importance of investing in the higher education was his key takeaway from MCC's site-selection competition. At the time, Texas made a big commitment to higher education and the states that lost the MCC competition took note.

"I got letters out of California later telling me I did more for the UC System by not coming than I ever would have done if we'd gone to San Diego," Inman said.

That's a lesson worth remembering.

▶ Buildings downtown

Photo by Ed Malcik

Chapter III: Brokering Peace

◀◀ Paddlers near Barton Springs
Photo by Noah Towery

▲ The Buffalo represented here was once treasured in the western plains
Photo by Noah Towery

By the time I was elected mayor in 1997, the business community and environmentalists had been at war for years.

"Everything revolved around that conflict," said Toby Futrell, who was an assistant city manager during my tenure as mayor and later served as city manager.

At the center of that fight was Barton Springs.

Nestled in a corner of Zilker Park, Barton Springs feeds a beautiful, cool-water swimming hole very close to the heart of the city. Some say it is the soul of the Austin. Urban myth has it that the springs keep the pool at a constant, year-round 68 degrees (actually, the temperature varies, but just a little), which is incredibly refreshing on a scorching summer day in Texas. The springs and pool are also home to the endangered Barton Springs salamander.

Old Austin's music and culture "lived and breathed at the springs," said George Cofer, a leader in the effort to protect Barton Springs and its source, the Edwards Aquifer.

As Austin began to grow rapidly, Barton Springs faced a significant threat from intense development over the aquifer. When Freeport-McMoRan Inc. proposed at 4,000-acre development along Barton Creek, hundreds of people packed into an all-night City Council hearing to oppose it. Much to everyone's surprise, they won.

Barton Springs "was in danger of being destroyed on our watch and people just weren't going to have that. They wanted to preserve it for themselves and future generations," said Daryl Slusher, a firebrand journalist elected to the Austin City Council in 1996.

That hearing in 1990 marked the moment that the environmental community discovered its political muscle. Two years later, voters circumvented the City Council and overwhelmingly approved the Save Our Springs ordinance, which imposed strict water-quality rules for development over the aquifer.

But the developers had their own muscle at the Texas Capitol, where state lawmakers became a rump appellate court and passed legislation that allowed development projects to go forward under the previous weaker rules. The Legislature so frequently targeted Austin and its efforts to protect its local decision-making and

HELLO. IS IT
OUR COURTYARD
YOU'RE LOOKING
FOR?
50 YEARS
OF LOVE
AND LIBERATION
HAPPY PRIDE

sense of place that the practice was given a name: "Austin Bashing".

Futrell noted that even as the Legislature was claiming that Austin's development rules were too onerous, Austin had more site plans being pulled than any other city in the state. Development was booming, she said, and Austinites were "desperately trying to preserve what they cherished about the community. At the heart of that was the environment."

So on any given Thursday, both sides could be found mixing it up at City Council public hearings where no one was hearing much of anything, just yelling and fighting.

"We were sucking every bit of oxygen out of City Hall," Cofer said. "It was just a general, constant, all-hands-on-deck oppose everything."

This became a de facto two-party system and was just as nasty, bitter and divisive as a partisan conflict between Democrats and Republicans. And it played out like the last minute of a basketball game when it's all about the foul — you're not trying to score, you're just trying to stop the other team from getting what it wants.

The constant fighting was tearing the city apart.

In Pursuit of Détente

Moving the city past that stalemate was a key part of my campaign for mayor. I maintained that Austin had an intellect big enough to wrap its head around more than two sides of an issue.

In fact, after spending a lot of time talking to folks, it was clear to me that the two sides actually agreed on some fundamental issues. Clean water and open-space preservation were essential to both of them but for very different reasons.

For the environmentalists, protecting water quality and endangered species' habitat was key to maintaining Austin's beautiful, unique natural character. For the business community, those factors were key to attracting and retaining talented people who could work anywhere but enjoyed that same beautiful, unique natural character.

While they were saying similar things, they weren't hearing each other. I thought I could help them find new ways of hearing because I already had experience working with folks on both sides.

In 1991, I was appointed by Governor Ann Richards to serve as the chairman of the Texas Air Control Board, the Texas agency responsible for air quality. Among other things, I worked with the East Austin community to shut down a gasoline tank farm and created a task force on environmental racism, the first of its kind at the time, along with my counterpart at the Texas Water Commission. I'd also served on the board of the Texas chapter of the Environmental Defense Fund.

And I'd had a stint with the Greater Austin Chamber of Commerce as the vice chair of government relations where I assisted with economic development activities.

I was also determined — some might say impatient — to make a lasting difference for my community. I'd spent the previous few years living through surgeries and chemotherapy for metastatic testicular cancer, and when doctors declared me cancer-free in 1995, I discovered a sense of freedom and urgency to do some things I'd always found a reason not to. The next year, at age 38, I launched my run for mayor.

Whatever plan I had to broker peace got tossed out the window not long after I took office in June 1997. The Legislature had inadvertently repealed the provision of code that had grandfathered all those properties from the Save Our Springs Ordinance, meaning the development over the aquifer would now be subject to the tight water-quality rules enacted by voters in 1992.

Developers insisted that the change was just a mistake and the city should go about its business as if nothing had changed. The environmental community, fresh off a clean sweep in the City Council election, now had a consensus "Green Council" and wasn't eager to compromise.

From my perspective at the center of the Green Council, any sort of environmental victory would be short-lived if we took a hard-line position. The Legislature would come back in 1999 and no doubt re-enact the grandfathering provisions and a whole lot more.

But maybe, just maybe, we could avoid the wrath of the Legislature by finding a workable solution for both sides.

The window for action was very short because the repeal would go into effect within a couple months and our normal ordinance-making process involving multiple boards and commissions wouldn't suffice. It was too diffuse, and no one could be held accountable if nothing happened. If we were going to fail, I thought I should be held responsible.

I quickly pulled together a 12-person "focus group" made up of six representatives each from the environmental and development communities, with the aim that they would make a recommendation to a council task force made up of two council members, Daryl Slusher and Gus Garcia and me. We would then take it to the full City Council.

We were starting from a position where neither side had any trust in the other and that shaped the process for our discussion. The task force met in public and the members made their points by talking to a mediator rather than directly confronting each other. It was the first step in creating a new way for members of the warring factions to hear each other.

At first, they just needed to vent. But eventually they got to the meat of the issue. Those of us from the City Council sat in on the discussions but mostly listened and asked questions.

The result was an ordinance that split the city into two areas — the Drinking Water Protection Zone and the Desired Development Zone — that were based largely on the distinctive geology of the area. The Austin Tomorrow Plan had laid out a similar construct back in the late 1970s.

Within the Drinking Water Protection Zone, we maintained strong regulatory safeguards to protect our most fragile water resources. And we lured development away from the aquifer to the Desired Development Zone by providing incentives, such as reduced fees, for projects that located in our moribund downtown or elsewhere in the urban core. This became a key part of our larger Smart Growth initiative.

"We made people on both sides mad, but what we did was a prudent result," Slusher said.

◀ South Congress offers a fun and open vibe.

Photo by Noah Towery

▶ The Barton Springs Pool is considered the crown jewel of Austin.

Photo by Kelly West

I've taken some heat over the years for both the process and the outcome. Neighborhood groups, in particular, didn't feel that they had a voice. Some people blame Smart Growth for a lot of change that had nothing to do with Smart Growth. Others say it has had the unintended consequence of hastening gentrification in East Austin, which was part of the Desired Development Zone. I'll get into that complicated question more in a later chapter.

Twenty years later, I still believe it was a good outcome under a very challenging set of circumstances, and it laid the groundwork for some cooperation that's had lasting and far-reaching benefits for the whole community.

The Three E's

I often heard developers rail against the Save Our Springs Ordinance and suggest that, if the city was going to regulate development over the aquifer so tightly, the city should just buy the land. They may have been more sarcastic than serious, but they had a point. After all, the only sure way to preserve that beneficial and treasured land was, well, to own it.

This concept wasn't new for Austin. In 1992, voters approved bonds to purchase land in western Travis County to preserve open space and habitat for endangered

species. The Balcones Canyonlands Preserve, a joint effort between the city, county and private partners, now has more than 31,000 acres under protection.

For the water quality lands, the idea was to buy land over the aquifer either in fee simple or through conservation easements where we would negotiate limited uses of the land. For example, land that had been a family farm or ranch could remain that way with specified houses, barns and sheds, but the development rights beyond those negotiated limits would be owned by the city.

We worked closely with our professional city staff to identify land that, from a scientific standpoint, would best protect the aquifer and water quality. With the help of The Nature Conservancy in Texas, the city started putting aquifer land under option long before we went public. We knew the price of land would go up as soon as we announced the plan to ask voters to authorize $65 million in bonds for some 15,000 acres of water-quality land.

At the same time, some folks in the business community were looking to expand the Austin Convention Center in downtown, creating an opportunity to bring together some of those longtime foes to support a bond package in May 1998 that would be mutually beneficial.

▶▶ George Cofer of the Hill Country Conservancy has played a key role in protecting Barton Springs.

Photo by Kelly West

▼ A Grackle in the Treaty Oak

Photo by Ed Malcik

I was still having to work both sides to get them to come together, but I had far more credibility as someone who was seeking common ground, trying to allow both sides to find a win and listening. Even so, I wasn't exactly sure what would happen with Gary Valdez, the chair of the Greater Austin Chamber of Commerce, and Robin Rather, the president of the Save Our Springs Alliance, sharing the stage at our press conference to announce the bond package. I was pretty sure they'd show up, but I didn't know exactly what they'd say. Later they joked that I made them shake hands. Those two were both important advisors to me and instrumental to helping our city move forward. They were strong, trusted advocates for their constituencies, but they were also empathetic leaders willing to listen.

A third piece of the bond package addressed the serious infrastructure needs on the east side of town where neighborhoods faced threats of flooding. We promoted them all together as the Three E's: environment, economic development and equity. All three passed with ease.

The night of the bond election, Rather told the *Austin Chronicle* that the passage of the bonds signaled a sea change in the community.

"I think what we're seeing is more coalition-building," she said. "The anger is dwindling."

By the following spring, the Greater Austin Chamber of Commerce, the Real Estate Council of Austin and the Save Our Springs Alliance had reached a peace agreement on environmental protection and development.

"It was a doozy of a challenge they undertook," the *Austin Chronicle* wrote, "but they did it (they being Save Our Springs Alliance, Real Estate Council of Austin, and the Greater Austin Chamber of Commerce): The odd bedfellows proved they could reach significant common ground, the kind that has the potential to bring positive change to a long-deadlocked area of Austin's public life."

Together, we went to the Texas Capitol during the 1999 legislative session to make the case that the Legislature didn't need to reinstate the controversial grandfathering legislation because we'd worked it out ourselves. Unfortunately, that argument didn't fly.

Despite the defeat at the Capitol, the whole dynamic had changed and people had gotten to know and respect each other, said David Armbrust, a development lawyer who led the Real Estate Council of Austin at the time.

And they followed through on the land conservation component of the peace agreement with the creation of a land trust, the Hill Country Conservancy, to protect 50,000 acres of open space over the aquifer.

Austin voters have repeatedly supported bonds to protect water protection land since that investment in 1998. And the people of San Antonio, who rely on the Edwards Aquifer for drinking water, have followed Austin's lead, as have the voters in three counties over the aquifer.

"As a group, voters in that entire region have authorized just under $1 billion," said Laura Huffman, state director of The Nature Conservancy in Texas. "It's huge. There's nothing on the planet like this in terms of that kind of systematic, scaled-up, voter-authorized investment in protecting water."

Austin Portrait: George Cofer, Executive Director of the Hill Country Conservancy

Photo by Kelly West

George Cofer meandered into his life's work.

The native lands and waters of Texas had played an integral role in Cofer's childhood growing up near Barton Springs in Austin, camping in the Hill Country and spending summers on a family cattle ranch along the Frio River in Uvalde County.

But he spent much of his adult life running a beer joint on Lake Austin and a remodeling company. He didn't pay attention to the politics and policy around land conservation until he got involved with the Save Barton Creek Association, when he was about 40.

"I walked off the street into this conversation. I'd been a hippie carpenter for a long time. I knew none of this," Cofer said.

The all-night City Council meeting in 1990 put Cofer on the front lines of the "aquifer wars" and, years later, at the table for the peace talks between business leaders and environmentalists. He's a laid-back person of passion, which gave him credibility with people on both sides and made him easy to work with. When those negotiations led to the creation of a land trust called the Hill Country Conservancy, the organization tapped Cofer to serve as its executive director.

At the first board meeting of the Hill Country Conservancy, the six environmentalists and six business leaders who served on the board were still wary of each other after years of conflict. To clear the air, Cofer brought a peace pipe for everyone to share.

Over the past two decades, the Hill Country Conservancy has done amazing work to preserve enormous swaths of open space in the Hill Country through outright purchases as well as conservation easements. Cofer's deep sense of what's right, combined with his quiet way of approaching people and his personal connection to ranching, has been particularly effective at finding common ground with the ranchers and other landowners who want to protect forever the Hill Country way of life — "keeping the Hill Country country," as Cofer puts it.

Cofer has taken the mission of the Hill Country Conservancy even further with the creation of the Violet Crown Trail, a regional trail system to connect urban wildlands. The Violet Crown trail is an ideal outcome from a guy like Cofer who has a vision and feels it in his gut that people and nature ought to be together.

Fender TELECASTER
Ludwig

◀ As the Live Music Capital of the World, Austin showcases an eclectic array of musical talents.

Photos by Erich Schlegel

Long before Gary Clark, Jr. became a Grammy-winning blues guitarist, he would sneak out of his parents' Austin home at night to take in the music downtown.

He wasn't old enough to get into a lot of clubs, but Clark said folks would let him in anyway because they knew he was truly interested in the music and the musicians. Whether it was blues, rockabilly, jazz, reggae, country or whatever, he soaked it all up and met pretty much every blues musician and guitar player in town, he said.

At age 15, Clark shared the stage at Antone's, one of Austin's early iconic music venues, with a group of blues legends, including Pinetop Perkins and James Cotton. He caught the eye of club owner Clifford Antone, a legend in his own right, who had been bringing the blues greats to town since 1975.

One of the neatest things about being Austin's mayor was the opportunity to shine a light on some of the wonderful people in our city. When I started hearing rumblings about this amazing young musician who was burning up the Austin music scene, I took the opportunity to proclaim May 3, 2001, as "Gary Clark Jr. Day" in Austin, Texas.

A junior at Austin High School at the time, Clark remembers wondering: "Are you sure you have the right guy? I'm just a kid."

"I didn't really know anybody was paying attention," he added. "That's really when I realized how music was important in the city."

Live Music Capital of the World

Stroll down South Congress Avenue late on a Wednesday and you're likely to catch singer-songwriter James McMurtry playing his regular midnight show at the Continental Club. No tickets required, just a small cover charge and great music is yours. Or come by on a Monday to hear The Peterson Brothers, two young blues and funk phenoms out of neighboring Bastrop County who I first saw at a school event when they were barely teenagers. They're on their way to becoming something big.

There's a reason we officially proclaimed ourselves to be the Live Music Capital of the World back in 1991. Music is everywhere. And it's a big part of how we see ourselves as a city and how others see us.

Down on the banks of Lady Bird Lake, there's a statue of a fellow that looks south across the park with the water at his back. It's not Sam Houston or Stephen F. Austin or some other Texan that put Austin on the map. No, it's someone who

▶▶ Willie Nelson's iconic performance at the Armadillo World Headquarters in 1972 marked the rise of the Austin music scene.

Photo by Sean Mathis

▼ Jonathan Tyler and Nikki Lane at the Continental Club

Photo by Sean Mathis

put Austin's music scene on the map — Stevie Ray Vaughan.

For Marcia Ball, who was named the 2018 Texas State Musician, Austin was supposed to be just a short stop between Louisiana and San Francisco in 1970. But a fortuitous bit of car trouble meant she was stuck in Austin for a few days and that was all it took.

"That was just it. I don't need to go anywhere else. I'd fallen in love with the town, with the ambiance, with the water, with the lakes," said Ball, an amazing Louisiana blues pianist and singer-songwriter.

She's been here ever since and remembers the wide array of music going on all over town back in the day. There was a good jazz scene. Stevie Ray Vaughan's band was playing clubs. On any given Wednesday, all the hippies would drop by an East Austin barbecue joint called Bonnie's for the band and then head to Kenneth Threadgill's North Austin gas station/bar/music venue that years before had been a favorite of Janis Joplin.

The disparate pieces of Austin music started to come together at the Armadillo World Headquarters, which opened in 1970.

Located in an old National Guard armory just south of the Colorado River, the Armadillo drew great talent and an appreciative audience that loved cold beer and good music.

"Everybody remembers 1972 as the year Willie Nelson first played the Armadillo, bringing out not only our usual crowd but also old died-in-the-wool C&W fans, including rednecks, who tended to be allergic to hippies and their environment," Armadillo co-founder Eddie Wilson writes in his book.

Willie Nelson had moved to town to get away from the industry in Nashville and came to embody the outlaw country movement that found a home at the Armadillo.

"He came back to Texas, for the gig money, for the familiarity of home turf, and for the belated Lone Star version of San Francisco that was going down in Austin," music writer and historian Joe Nick Patoski wrote. "Long hair and cowboy boots were suddenly cool. Beer and pot were held in equal regard. Recent arrivals including Doug Sahm, Michael Murphey, Jerry Jeff Walker, and Freda and the Firedogs were breaking down traditional music barriers. Rock and folk were sounding twangy. Country was morphing into something else."

Ball fronted Freda and the Firedogs and said playing the Armadillo was like Carnegie Hall for her up-and-coming band that had cut their teeth at honky-tonks, including the Broken Spoke and the Split Rail. I remember first seeing and hearing her at a hamburger joint called Hut's. She loved playing country music because "it was pretty and it had melodies and it had stories," and the Armadillo created a place where the hippies could make it their own.

The Armadillo closed after a decade, finally succumbing to the constant struggle to pay the bills. But it left an enduring legacy — and the foundation for the Live Music Capital of the World — by fostering the creativity of people who bucked conventional thinking.

As Willie once mused in song, "I'd have to be weird/to grow me a beard/just to see what the rednecks would do."

ACL & SXSW

For a lot of folks — and a lot of budding musicians — the first time they saw Austin was as the backdrop to the television show Austin City Limits, which started on the local public television station in the mid-1970s as a way to showcase the eclectic live music of the city. The skyline in the background featured the Texas Capitol, the University of Texas Tower and not much else, which is a pretty accurate picture of what Austin once was.

"It was an amazing portal to the world for Austin musicians, especially in the early days," said Ball, who has appeared on Austin City Limits five times and was inducted into the ACL Hall of Fame in 2018.

Even now, she says, people come up after her performances all over the country to say they'd never heard of her before seeing her on Austin City Limits.

It's now the longest-running music program in American television history and has expanded its brand to the Austin City Limits Music Festival, a radio station and a downtown music venue, Austin City Limits Live at The Moody Theater. A statue of Willie, who filmed the show's first episode and has appeared a record 18 times, sits outside the theater at 310 Willie Nelson Boulevard.

Others started hearing about Austin and its creative energy in 1987 with the launch of South By Southwest.

According to the official SXSW history, the founders believed "that the local creative and music communities were as talented as anywhere else on the planet but were severely limited by a lack of exposure outside of Austin."

What started as a music conference and festival has ballooned to now cover film, interactive, and so much more. They've certainly overcome that lack of outside exposure as hordes of people from all over the world come to town each spring for an ever-evolving event that covers a huge swath of downtown.

Even as it's evolved over the past 30-plus years, SXSW has stayed true to its original mission of giving creatives a forum to share what they're creating, said Mayor Steve Adler. But the creatives are now entrepreneurs that are coming up with new platforms and, instead of just record labels, they're pitching to venture capitalists.

Former Austin Mayor Lee Cooke, who played an instrumental role integrating music into the city's economic development strategy as president of the chamber of commerce in the '80s, said SXSW is one of the key reasons that Austin is on the international stage today. It's shown the world that ideas are Austin's greatest export.

"Alright, alright, alright"

Years ago, standing in the Austin home of Tobe Hooper, the director of "The Texas Chain Saw Massacre," I couldn't resist telling him about my, uh, "favorite" scene in his 1974 horror film classic that had been filmed all around Austin.

I was a fearless young college student when I'd seen the movie but the meat hook scene made me jump out of my seat. Hooper, who also directed "Poltergeist," listened intently to my story as I graphically described the terrifying scene he obviously knew very well. He had achieved the result he wanted — 20 years after seeing it, I was still haunted by the scene.

As I finished my story, he slowly reached over to a bookcase, and, with perfect timing, grabbed the hook and thrust it toward me.

He scared the heck out of me! Again. He was very proud — and rightfully so.

Talented, creative people really are all over the place in Austin, and they've given rise to a vibrant film scene.

In 1990, filmmaker Richard Linklater captured the Austin vibe with "Slacker," which showed "a day in life of Austin, Texas as the camera roams from place to place and provides a brief look at the over-educated, the social misfits, the outcasts and the oddballs."

Overeducated oddballs. I love it. That about sums us up.

Linklater offered another great look at Austin in his next defining production, "Dazed and Confused," which featured a 19th-century moonlight tower (not technically) as well as a UT student named Matthew McConaughey. Later, he made Austin home to "Boyhood."

Robert Rodriguez made his first feature film, "El Mariachi," in 1991 while still a student at the University of Texas. It cost him $7,000. In 1993, when the movie won the Audience Award at the Sundance Film Festival, Rodriguez already had a deal with Columbia Pictures and was plowing forward with his cutting-edge technology and unconventional production style.

He was told by George Lucas at one point to stay in Austin rather than go to Hollywood because when you live outside the box, you think outside the box.

"It's true. When you're out here, all the rules that they have in Hollywood just don't make any sense to you," Rodriguez said. "Let's just try it. Who's going to tell us we're doing it wrong?"

The late Governor Ann Richards played a role in planting the idea with Linklater and Rodriguez that one day Austin should reuse the hangars at the former Mueller Municipal Airport to make movies.

The decision had been made in 1991 to move airport operations a little farther southeast to the old Air Force base that was being decommissioned, but the airport didn't finally close until 1999. That's when we started working with the Austin filmmakers on a plan, developed with the Austin Film Society, to convert the old hangars into a production facility called Austin Studios.

The master plan to redevelop over 700 acres of airport land into a vibrant mixed-use development in the heart of Austin was well on its way to being complete. But Linklater and others worked closely with neighborhood groups and planners to make the studios a key anchor component of the development.

"We can build sets and we can draw a film industry here," Rodriguez said. "I don't want to leave so I'll just make all my movies here."

Sandra Bullock lived in Austin and made "Miss Congeniality" here using one

◀◀ Janis Joplin, who honed her voice in Austin as a University of Texas student, looks out over other performers.

Photo by Ed Malcik

▲ Every nook and cranny becomes a live music venue during SXSW — also know as South by Southwest.

Photo by Erich Schlegel

▶ Crowds fill the streets during SXSW each spring.

Photo by Erich Schlegel

of those hangars. You can see it in the background as her FBI agent character emerges as the beauty queen — and then falls down.

John Lee Hancock directed his first major picture "A Perfect World" with Clint Eastwood and Kevin Costner in and around Austin. He also shot "The Rookie" and "The Alamo" here.

Rodriguez set up shop for his Troublemaker Studios in a former state hangar that used to house the governor's plane. There he put in a green screen and began cranking out movies at an incredible pace, starting with "Spy Kids" and building toward his biggest production yet, "Alita: Battle Angel."

And staying outside the box has worked for Rodriguez.

"Still even after all these years you can feel the energy and the excitement because people don't live here to work, they work to live here," Rodriguez said.

LAKERS
32

Austin Portrait: Gary Clark, Jr.

Photo by Laura Skelding

Gary Clark, Jr., left Austin just as his career was positively exploding.

A 2010 appearance at Eric Clapton's Crossroad Guitar Festival led to a deal with a major label and the release of his debut record, "Blak and Blu." Clark started burning up the festival scene, hitting the international tour circuit, playing with the greats and picking up some prominent fans, such as President Barack Obama.

But the tug of his hometown — and his mama — pulled him back around the time that his son was born.

"I felt like a little bit of a traitor. I spent my whole life in this town that had kinda raised me, not just to be a musician, but to be a man," Clark said. "I don't want to turn my back on the place that lifted me up when everything started to heat up and there's a buzz here."

"The spotlight isn't going to last forever, and I don't want to keep it all myself," he added. "If I can spread it around and share the love, I'll be totally down to do that. That's a big reason I moved back to Austin."

Clark has invested in the resurgence of Antone's, the legendary blues club that nurtured him as he was coming up in the music scene. Clifford Antone, who opened the club in 1975, had changed Clark's life and giving new life to Antone's ensures there's a home for blues in Austin.

And he says his mind is moving about what more he can do to foster Austin music and help the scene evolve.

"We have something that's very important to music and to culture here. We have a certain voice," Clark said.

In early 2019, Clark dropped his latest record, "This Land." The title track is a raw and searing comment on race in America and has generated a lot of buzz.

Clark credits his success to his roots in Austin.

"I don't know what I would be, my whole thing would be different if I wasn't introduced to the Austin music scene. I don't know what I'd be doing," he said.

▲ Gary Clark Jr.

Photo by Laura Skelding

▲ Robert Rodriguez

Photo by Laura Skelding

Austin Portrait: Robert Rodriguez

Photo by Laura Skelding

Robert Rodriguez had been making movies since he was a kid in San Antonio, using his nine siblings as cast and crew.

When he came to Austin for college, Rodriguez continued making short films, but his grades kept him from getting into the University of Texas film program. Eventually, the professor relented when Rodriguez showed him that he was beating out the film students in local contests.

Rodriguez's real education in filmmaking, however, came when he set out on his own to make a feature film over summer break. He wanted to make a movie that looked big but he would do all the production jobs himself so it would be cheap. The result was "El Mariachi," which he sold to Columbia Pictures in 1992.

It was the classic demonstration of Rodriguez's penchant to do everything a little differently.

Rodriguez created his own studio, Troublemaker Studios, in Austin with a green-screen stage and has consistently pushed the envelope on technology. For example, he made the first digital 3-D movie, "Spy Kids 3", at a time when there were only two digital screens in the country.

He also launched an English-language television network, El Rey, to reach an underserved millennial Latinx audience. For the network, Rodriguez has developed original content including his own interview show, "The Director's Chair," a TV-series based on his 1996 cult classic, "From Dusk to Dawn," and a reality show where he tasked young filmmakers to make a movie on their own with $7,000 — just as he did with "El Mariachi."

The most ambitious endeavor so far for Troublemaker Studios has been the production of "Alita: Battle Angel," a futuristic action film written by James Cameron and released in early 2019.

The set for Iron City, the fictional setting of "Alita," stands tall in a parking lot outside Troublemaker Studios not far from Austin's very real downtown. The structure was built to last 15 years, Rodriguez said, and he intends to use it as the bones for future Troublemaker productions. It's a big-budget Hollywood investment that's staying in Austin.

Rodriguez, who is a remarkably prolific filmmaker, said he's been able to innovate and create in Austin in a way that wouldn't have been possible in Hollywood.

"It feels very free. If you can make something happen, you can make it happen here," Rodriguez said.

Chapter V: Austin's Living Room

Today, downtown Austin offers a little bit of everything. More than 12,000 people call downtown home as do a wide array of businesses — among them the flagship store of the homegrown Whole Foods.

We have welcoming public spaces, including the hike-and-bike trail along Lady Bird Lake and urban parks that host the farmers market, movie nights and free live music. There's life on the streets all the time with sidewalk cafes, retail shops, bars and restaurants.

In 2018, *Time Magazine* named the new Austin Central Library one of the World's Greatest Places.

Downtown "is your living room. It's how you present yourself to the world," said Jesus Garza, who served as city manager during my time as mayor. "If you have a dead downtown, when the world comes to see you, that's what they see. But if you have a vibrant, really electric downtown, the world sees a lot of vitality."

For many, many decades, Austin presented folks with an aged, crumbling downtown that was dull and lifeless, particularly after 5 p.m. when the lawyers, bankers and state employees went home.

Lee Cooke remembers coming to Austin in the early '70s for a job with Texas Instruments.

"What you saw downtown was left over from the 1890s. You had warehouses and railroad tracks from another economic era. That's what downtown was in the 1970s. It was dying," Cooke said.

When Cooke joined the Austin City Council in 1977, he teamed up with Mayor Carole Keeton to address some of the serious infrastructure troubles in downtown, including the stormwater runoff that regularly flooded Congress Avenue shops. They also widened the sidewalks, planted trees along Congress Avenue and encouraged the building owners to tear down the ugly facades that had been put up in the '30s and '40s and restore the original buildings.

All told, the city invested heavily in downtown to lay the foundation for what was to come.

"It was the beginning of the beginning of the beginning," Cooke said.

Lighting the Spark

In 1973, the City of Austin picked up several prime downtown blocks for a steal. Legend has it that Mayor Roy Butler was helping out a friend by taking the land off his hands. Butler had designs on putting a new City Hall on the property between First Street (now Cesar Chavez Street) and Second Street overlooking Town Lake, what we now call Lady Bird Lake.

◀◀ The Texas State Capitol by night

Photo by Erich Schlegel

◀ Community First! Village offers a Friday night movie for anyone to enjoy.

Photo by Sam Cole

GOOD HUMOR
Breyers
KLONDIKE
SPECIALIZED

◀ The Austin Convention Center sits on the eastern edge of downtown.

Photo by Casey Dunn, courtesy of Page

▲ The Texas Book Festival takes over the Texas Capitol and the nearby streets each fall.

Photo by Erich Schlegel

The city converted the Calcasieu Lumber Company building to serve as the temporary council chambers. The City Council was still operating out of those "temporary" chambers when I was elected mayor in 1997. And the area around it, much of it also city owned, looked abandoned.

An old warehouse immediately east of the council chambers and proposed City Hall site had a big tree growing up in the middle of it and we just treated that as normal. That same block housed some of the city staff that dealt with land development. The building was a constant source of complaint, by city employees and the public who went to do business there, because of the rats.

The block just west was the home to the J.P. Schneider Store. This brick structure was built in 1873 and had housed the first dry goods store that folks crossing the river from the south would encounter as they came into Austin proper. Rather than doing something with that historic building, the city boarded it up.

A little further to the west was a water treatment plant, the Seaholm Power Plant and a pole yard for Austin Energy — yeah, we were storing poles on the edge of our Central Business District.

I used to tell folks, "If you walk through your downtown and point out the ugliest property, you probably own it." All of it was unsightly and none of it was on the tax roll.

Breathing new life into this swath of city-owned waterfront property was a key recommendation from the Regional/Urban Design Assistance Team (R/UDAT) from the American Institute of Architects, when they first came to Austin in 1991 at the behest of then-Mayor Lee Cooke and others.

Downtown Austin had been hit particularly hard by the collapse of the savings and loan industry and the real estate bust a few years earlier. Though a few new downtown office towers had gone up in the late-1980s, demand had plummeted and left several vacant, "see-through" buildings.

"Downtown was moribund," said Charlie Betts, the retired executive director of the Downtown Austin Alliance. "It was really a grim time."

R/UDAT helped the community develop a downtown vision but little came of it in the intervening years, beyond the creation of the downtown public improvement district and the Downtown Austin Alliance.

In 1997, working with several advocates for downtown, I brought R/UDAT back to revisit their recommendations.

▲ The Austin Central Library has been named one of the World's Greatest Places by *Time Magazine.*

Photo by Winston O'Neal for CCR Press

One of those recommendations was a new performing arts center, which we accomplished quickly through a great public/private partnership. The city supplied the property on the south shore of Town Lake, thanks to the voters in 1998, and turned a sea of asphalt into lakefront parkland.

And the arts community raised the money — over $60 million — through philanthropy to retrofit the aging Palmer Events Center into a new, first-class arts center. Today, we have the Long Center for the Performing Arts, named after major benefactors Joe and Teresa Lozano Long, as well as a new Palmer Events Center.

R/UDAT's top recommendation was the redevelopment of the city's waterfront properties. They saw it as an opportunity for mixed-use residential along with public uses, including City Hall.

But where to start? Experts were saying we needed more retail downtown before private developers would build housing downtown, but to get private developers to build retail we needed more residential. We had a chicken-and-egg problem.

So, we decided to forge ahead ourselves and created a public-private partnership with Post Properties to build a 200-unit residential project downtown on that pole yard. Clearly, there was a demand because it leased up faster than anyone expected.

"If the private sector wasn't doing it, the private sector doesn't believe it can be done," said Molly Alexander, executive director of the Downtown Austin Alliance Foundation. "They're not going to make a move and build in a market unless it's proven. So how do you help them prove that? Well, you become their partner. The city became their partner and proved up the market very fast."

Living downtown but without a home

Of course, a large number of Austinites were already living in downtown — on the streets, under Interstate Highway 35, in the woods along the hike-and-bike trail. And we needed to create a place where our neighbors could rest, eat a meal, and find comfort.

A task force had been working on identifying a good site somewhere in Austin to place a shelter or resource center. But each time the task force would get close to naming a site, the choice would get leaked to the newspaper, there would be a front-page article, the neighborhood or area that felt threatened would howl and the task force would go back to the drawing board.

When I was first elected mayor, the resource center for the homeless was co-located with the day labor site in a sad, run-down building on part of those waterfront properties that we purchased almost 25 years before for a new city hall and other updated development. There was no good reason to co-locate those two uses other than the sad reality was the city wasn't dealing with either issue well.

The task force approach wasn't working. The status quo of doing nothing wasn't working. Something needed to give. I held a press conference in 1998 saying we were starting over. I didn't have a solution. I didn't have a place for a shelter. But something new had to happen.

One of the city's leading philanthropists, Dick Rathgeber, pitched the idea of an emergency shelter near the current Salvation Army in downtown. There was already a shelter there and the people we needed to serve gravitated to where others were. So, after some initial due diligence and with some good old-fashioned hope, I started pursuing this site and took the idea public.

"This is the only place a shelter can go without raising a firestorm of protest," Rathgeber told the *Austin Chronicle* in 1999. "Some people in this city would like to see them somewhere between Midland and Marathon."

I was amazed, and I remain amazed, at how many folks insisted that the twin goals for downtown — a vibrant place for people to work, live and play and providing relief for our homeless neighbors — were mutually exclusive. They presented it as the worst sort of zero-sum game: take care of your city — as they defined the city — or take care of the homeless. And I don't need to tell you which part of that equation those folks were cheering for.

We had to beat back the strong, orchestrated, well-financed effort to sweep up the homeless and dump them elsewhere where they could be guiltlessly ignored and forgotten.

We did a lot of work addressing needs of those living in homelessness when I was mayor. I'm still proud of it. We shifted thinking and focused on the creation of a continuum of services. We made a multi-million-dollar infusion of funding for what was then known as SafePlace to assist women and children. We created a special downtown court to help those charged with nuisance violations to find help. We also empowered and formed lasting partnerships with non-profits and faith-based groups that are still doing so much to address this daily tragedy.

And we built the Austin Resource Center for the Homeless, which opened in 2004. It was intended to be a first step, a temporary place for a person to get resources and then be able to move into a more permanent situation. By that time, I'd left

▼ A little boy peers out the window of an East Austin barber shop.

Photo by John Langmore

▶▼ East Austin

Photo by Noah Towery

the Mayor's office and that essential next step fell by the wayside.

At the time, I knew we were making progress and hoped more would be made, but I also felt like this city never wrapped its arms around the issue of homelessness and those who are homeless as it should.

Little has changed over the past 20 years. Work — some of it good work — continues. But when the issue blew up in 2019, the community conversation was much of the same, only nastier because now there's social media.

The problem has grown worse. The city government simply must do more than speak in legalistiic and moralistic platitudes. There needs to be less talk and more action, for certain. But as members of this community we all need to recognize that the folks experiencing homelessness are our neighbors, too, and having people living on the downtown streets and under bridges along IH 35 is a failure of humanity and our community.

Growing Smarter

Drawing development away from the sensitive aquifer land — the Drinking Water Protection Zone — and into the Desired Development Zone was key to addressing the aquifer politics that had dominated Austin for years.

And the most desired area of the Desired Development Zone was downtown. After all, downtown was already developed so no new land would be affected and we also had the essential infrastructure in place.

We couldn't stop growth, but we could manage it by discouraging suburban sprawl with all its environmental, social and fiscal implications and encouraging folks to go to where we wanted them to go. Our Smart Growth program was intended to be the carrot.

We offered incentives, such as fee waivers and expedited approval, to developers who were willing to build in the Desired Development Zone and tailor their project to the city's guidelines for green-building standards, streetscape improvements, affordable housing, mixed uses and more.

We didn't write checks to the developers but waived some fees that the city wouldn't have been collecting but for the project. And by encouraging development in downtown where we already had infrastructure in place, we were coming out ahead compared to the cost of suburban greenfield development.

Perry Lorenz, who developed the first Smart Growth project, said the $280,000 fee abatement was very small piece of the $36 million multi-family project, the

▲ The Second Street District helped spark the renaissance of Austin's downtown

Photo by Casey Dunn, courtesy of Page

Brewed Coffee
Espresso
242
Mocha
Chai Latte
Iced Coffee
Hot Chocolate
Hot Teas
Iced Teas
ICED
MON-FRI

Nokonah. The most valuable part of the deal was the partnership with the city, he said.

"Psychologically, it gets you on the same side as the city so the city is pulling for you. They want you to look good," Lorenz said.

In 1999, I got a call one day that Computer Sciences Corporation was planning to locate a sprawling suburban campus in Austin — directly over the aquifer. That could have been a nightmare.

Instead, we turned it into an opportunity to lure a major employer away from the Drinking Water Protection Zone and into the Desired Development Zone. And we had some downtown city land to use as bait — a few of those virtually dormant blocks that the city had purchased back in 1973.

We put on the hard sell, traveling to California to sit down with the CEO of Computer Sciences Corporation. He really wanted a suburban campus so I countered with a "campus" across the street from a lake and a hike-and-bike trail that is second to none.

WE CONVINCED THEM.

"It was all just negotiation and persuasion and appealing to them to comply with community will and that worked," said Daryl Slusher, one of my City Council colleagues.

For our downtown to thrive, we needed the new economy to live and work there. We needed what was happening in Austin to be reflected in our downtown. I even tried calling it "Austin 3D," the Digital Downtown District. The name never caught on but the idea did, eventually. And the CSC decision to come downtown was a turning point because other tech companies followed its lead.

CSC prepaid a 99-year lease for three of the downtown blocks while the city maintained ownership. The cash from the prepayment enabled us finally to build our new City Hall in the heart of the new Second Street retail district that included ground-floor retail, residential and commercial uses on what had been a downtown dead zone.

In the end, CSC turned one of the blocks back over to the city, which opened up a location for the W Hotel and a new home for Austin City Limits. A few blocks away, the site of the former water treatment plant provided a home for the new Austin Central Library and the adjacent Seaholm Power Plant became a mixed-used development anchored by a Trader Joe's. In 2005, CSC sold its lease to Austin's own Silicon Labs, which maintains its headquarters in the builldings now.

Our Smart Growth initiative certainly had its troubles, too. The deals we negotiated to bring Intel and Vignette downtown both famously blew up. The partially built shell of the Intel building stood until 2007 when it was imploded to make room for the new federal courthouse.

There were also some casualties. Most notable was Liberty Lunch, a live music venue that had picked up the mantle after the Armadillo World Headquarters closed. Liberty Lunch was the first place I heard live music in Austin. I was still in law school and a buddy of mine that I'd met way back when we were both debating in high school was clerking for a law firm during a summer. He called and told me I just had to come hear a group called Beto y Los Fairlanes.

When Liberty Lunch was set to close to make room for CSC on the block just west of the new City Hall, the *Austin American-Statesman* wrote about what made Liberty Lunch iconic: "The sound wasn't that good, the architecture simply unimpressive. No A/C; no matter: There wasn't any insulation, and at one time no

▼ The piñata selection in Austin can't be beat.

Photo by Noah Towery

▶▶ Tattoo artists take a break downtown.

Photo by Noah Towery

roof. But the beer was cheap and always cold. And roof or not, when that shed was kickin', $7 would buy an intimate evening with the Dave Matthews Band, the Smashing Pumpkins, Nirvana or countless other then-nobodies who were real close to becoming somebodies. And most of them did."

We had worked tirelessly to help the owner of Liberty Lunch relocate and even provided a loan. It didn't matter. When Liberty Lunch closed for good, folks burned a photo of me in effigy. That one still hurts.

To the East

There were big plans for the other end of Second Street, too.

The Austin Convention Center, which sits next to Waller Creek on the eastern edge of downtown, had opened in 1992 and folks were already looking to expand it by 1998.

But the flooding of Waller Creek had long been a problem.

"The creek has always had the potential to be a corridor of beauty through an otherwise heavily paved area of town, but has instead become a forgotten and neglected ditch," the *Austin Chronicle* wrote in 1998.

It was a festering puncture wound in downtown, and we used a few different approaches to stop the spread of the infection. Some were better than others.

As I mentioned earlier, our 1998 bond election focused on The Three E's: environment, economic development and equity. The economic development piece focused on doubling the size of the convention center and $25 million to build a tunnel as a water control project to address the flooding on Waller Creek, which would open up that swath of downtown for redevelopment.

The expanded convention center and a related public-private hotel project allowed Austin to host much larger conventions. Both were resounding successes.

The flood-control tunnel, not so much. The engineering report that led to our cost estimate for the tunnel was dead wrong and we didn't have anywhere near enough to complete the project at the time.

But folks never gave up on the vision for Waller Creek and it's finally coming to fruition. A $163 million tunnel project provides flood protection for 28 acres of prime downtown land and has opened up an amazing opportunity to restore the stream ecosystem and create the Waterloo Greenway along the creek.

The first piece is Waterloo Park, which is set for completion in 2020. It'll include an outdoor amphitheater and ample green space in the shadow of the Texas Capitol. A few blocks away, the state is building an urban greenspace akin to the National Mall in Washington, D.C. that will open an area as grand as the Capitol building itself.

It's going to be a pretty special place.

Austin Portrait: Molly Alexander

executive director of the Downtown Austin Alliance Foundation

Photo by Kelly West

Downtown is much more than a central location for Molly Alexander. It's a shared place that tells the story of a community and draws people together on common ground.

For her day job, Alexander runs the Downtown Austin Alliance Foundation, a newly created non-profit focused on preserving cultural and historical spaces in downtown and making public spaces there inviting for everyone. She was with the Downtown Austin Alliance for 15 years, ultimately serving as executive vice president of economic development, before launching the foundation.

She sees opportunities to collaborate with live music venues, artists, community groups and local officials to shape the shared space in order to enhance it and assure it remains vibrant, engaging and accessible as downtown grows. The goal is to rethink the public space and to invest in making it truly for the public.

"My whole life's purpose is building community," Alexander said. "For me, building community in downtown aligned my love of history (and) my love of seeing how people interact and come together to celebrate."

Alexander continues her community-building when she goes home to Elgin, a small town located about 20 miles from Austin known for its sausage and the annual pig-themed Hogeye Festival.

She and her partner, Gary Luedecke, co-own two small businesses on Main Street in Elgin's historic downtown. The Owl Wine Bar & Home Goods Store opened in 2012 in a beautiful old building featuring an original ghost mural of Owl Cigars, circa 1900. The idea was to create a space close to home where locals could come to enjoy a glass of wine, linger and shop. She knew there was a demand for social spaces in town but at the time, there were only a few businesses on Main Street. It was a bit of a risk but a risk worth taking.

"If everyone wants it, and we want it too, then don't we have a responsibility to try it? Six years later, it is supporting itself...And we really feel that it's helped revitalize downtown Elgin," Alexander said.

In 2014, The Owl was named the Best Downtown Business by the Texas Downtown Association and the pair has followed up with G&M Drygoods, a unique gift shop just down the street.

Now, there are businesses up and down Main Street.

▲ Molly Alexander

Photo by Kelly West

▲ Residents of Community First! Village make a variety of creations in the Community Art House.

Photo by Kelly West

Austin Portrait: Alan Graham

Founder & Chief Executive Officer of Mobile Loaves & Fishes

Photo by Kelly West

God has given Alan Graham some pretty good ideas.

It started with a catering truck and a mission to start feeding people on the streets. Together with some friends from St. John Neumann Catholic Church, Graham launched Mobile Loaves & Fishes in 1998 and began a ministry of service to the men and women experiencing homelessness in Austin.

Graham spent time getting to know the people on the streets and developing deep personal relationships.

"It was in this process that I began to learn that the single greatest cause of homelessness was a profound, catastrophic loss of family," Graham said.

He came to believe that housing alone wouldn't solve homelessness, but community could.

In 2005, Graham bought a gently used RV to lift one person off the streets and put it in a private RV park. That gave Graham his next big idea — "an RV park on steroids."

Community First! Village is a 27-acre community that opened in 2015 for more than 200 men and women coming out of chronic homelessness. It features tiny houses and RVs, beautiful gardens, communal kitchens, and an outdoor movie theatre that offers a Friday night public screening. Everyone pays rent and the on-site microenterprises — such as the bed and breakfast operation, art studio, blacksmithing and car care facility — enable the residents to earn an income.

About 20 percent of the residents, including the president of a tech company and professors from University of Texas, live at Community First! Village as "missional" residents. And hundreds of people from outside the community itself come through every week to enjoy the movies, shop at the Community Market, stay in the Airbnb rentals or volunteer.

"This is the most diverse neighborhood in Austin, Texas, right here," Graham said. "And the most talked about neighborhood in Austin, Texas."

The second phase, which will more than double the capacity for residents, is set to open in late 2019 and will include a healthcare facility, respite care center, outdoor events space and more.

At the heart of it all is community.

Austin
ROAD CLOSED
ROAD WORK AHEAD
ROAD WORK AHEAD
DETOUR

Chapter VI: Gridlock

NOTHING — NOT THE MUSIC, THE SUMMER HEAT OR EVEN UT FOOTBALL — GENERATES MORE CHATTER IN THIS TOWN THAN THE TRAFFIC.

Everyone loves to hate all of our congested roadways, but the most disliked is Interstate Highway 35, the north-south thoroughfare that cuts through all of Texas and has dWivided Austin for far too long. It's ugly and outdated and traffic is often at a virtual standstill. It's also a cultural, historical and economic scar that we need to eradicate in order to reconnect our city and improve access to healthcare, education and jobs.

For some of us, our mobility challenge is inconvenient and frustrating. But for others, it's a roadblock to a productive future as well as a roadblock to happiness because it forces unwanted changes in the way people live.

There's plenty of blame to go around for why we haven't been able to solve this problem over the decades.

For many years, the local resistance to growth led to the mindset of "if you don't build it, they won't come." They came anyway, and I joked (sort of) when I was first elected mayor that I was declaring a winner in that debate: No one. We all lost. We grew but didn't have the infrastructure we needed to manage the growth wisely.

Austin and its suburbs grew initially along the north-south axes created by I-35 to the east and a state highway to the west that is almost universally known as "MoPac" because it generally parallels the Missouri Pacific rail line. The fight to build MoPac, which opened in 1975, was a big one. But it's hard to imagine getting around Austin today without it.

Population and traffic growth have had an impact on MoPac, resulting in a dark humor Twitter handle @EvilMopacATX that gives voice to the frustration. The road has recently been improved and expanded with the region's first managed lane along with sound walls to protect neighborhoods next to the high-capacity road. The managed lanes have helped to increase transit ridership in the corridor by 65%.

When I arrived in Austin and for many years after, the big debate was about building an east-west thoroughfare cutting across what was then the central part

◀ The community is working together to reduce traffic congestion; it's a long term battle.

Photos by Noah Towery

▲ "Forever Bicycles" by Ai Weiwei made a temporary home near the Waller Creek Boathouse.

Photo by Ed Malcik

of Austin. The road never was built because it would have done legitimate damage to a number of neighborhoods. But the flip side is that by not building such a designated path, many more neighborhoods have been affected because folks have to try to get across town somehow, so they cut through the neighborhoods on streets not meant for such capacity. The city's response has been speed humps and other traffic calming devices. In other words, slowing traffic even more.

The State of Texas has also been an unreliable partner in addressing our transportation challenges. We've had many, many efforts to improve I-35 over the years, especially through downtown Austin — they have, shall we say, been false starts. In addition, those in control of the Capitol simply refuse to allow state dollars to be invested in mass transit. In the Capitol, rail is a four-letter word and buses are something the feds invest in, not the state. It's a terribly short-sighted policy that, unfortunately, isn't changing anytime soon.

And our community has tried — and failed — twice to approve light rail referenda. In 2000, we lost by fewer than 2,000 votes.

My City Council colleague Daryl Slusher said the 2000 light rail loss was the single most disappointing experience during this tenure in office.

"That one hurts me," Slusher said.

If we had won, we'd be talking about expanding light rail today, and I believe we'd have forestalled lots of problems over the past two decades. Our lack of some key mass transit infrastructure, and even our failure to build more road infrastructure has exacerbated gentrification in the neighborhoods close to downtown. People are willing to pay more for housing near the central business district because it's too hard to travel from the suburbs. That infrastructure failure has contributed to the escalating costs in close-in neighborhoods, pushing people farther and farther away in pursuit of lower-cost housing options only to face increased transportation costs and a lot of time lost sitting in traffic.

We've known for 40 years that we need a mass transit system to "complement" our roadways but haven't been able to get it done. We've been stymied by the polarized debate over roads vs. rail. At times, we've even seen transit advocates at war with each other over the "best" way to do it. But I'm hopeful that we're about to overcome those divisions to ensure that folks from throughout the community can access the bounty of economic opportunities wherever they are located.

Current estimates are for 4 million people to call Central Texas home by 2040. If we don't do something now, our quality

▲ Bark 'n Purr

Photo by Ed Malcik

of life will only deteriorate. And more hardworking Austinites will be forced to move far away from their jobs with no other alternative than to add their cars on already congested roads.

It's time to do this right. We need to go big or we're done for.

Reconnection

We have a vision for I-35 that could serve our economic needs while also reflecting the values of our community. It's big and bold, but it's not cheap.

Since 2011, I've been working with neighborhood leaders, business groups, downtown interests, state transportation planners and others to develop a plan for I-35 that not only improves mobility on the highway, including with the use of transit, but also allows us to tie our community together, both literally and figuratively.

That vision includes lowering I-35 in downtown Austin to allow us one day to cap portions of the highway and perhaps build a park on top, as Dallas has done with Klyde Warren Park, as a way to connect East Austin and West Austin. It also calls for a smarter approach to managing traffic, including giving transit reliable access to downtown from the edges of the service area.

Our state leaders, playing politics, have failed to support funding sources sufficient to even maintain the state's current congestion, much less accommodate future growth in Texas. That makes big projects very hard.

They pay lip service to reducing congestion in our cities but, more often than not, throw up roadblocks instead. It's been disappointing, but the plan is too good and the need too big to give up.

▲ The launch of the Transit for Austin coalition in 2019

Photo by Jovita Pardo

▶ Flag of the Lone Star State

Photo by Erich Schlegel

LITTLE STAR
CRUISES
CrystalKayak
WERNER

At the height of the dot-com boom in 1999, University of Texas at Austin President Larry Faulkner sat on a panel at a gathering of Austin's high-tech entrepreneurs called the 360 Summit. He'd been cast as the defender of the status quo while Andrew Heller, an IBM alum and technology consultant, was the figurative barbarian at the gate.

The 360 Summit was part of the youthful (some might say, immature) tech community's attempt to prove it was the New Economy and in control of business. The invitation-only 360 Summit was a flashy, expensive event held at the Four Seasons Hotel complete with ping pong tables in the hallways and other artifices of being cutting-edge.

David Gibson of the IC² Institute said there was a lot of hubris among that crowd at the time.

"Too much money, not enough talent, not enough awareness," Gibson said.

At that first summit in 1999, the organizers provided the audience members with Wiffle balls to serve as "feedback devices." If the audience members didn't like something they heard, they had the balls at the ready and were encouraged to throw them at the offending speaker.

UT President Faulkner made the case that universities have tremendous staying power because they're adaptable. Let's not forget that the University of Texas was a huge factor in the recruitment of MCC and much of the tech industry that followed. He noted that the University of Texas had been thriving for well over a century and would continue to evolve.

There was some give and take between Faulkner and some audience members who thought their ideas and businesses were more important to the Austin economy than a top-tier research university. Faulkner, a PhD in Chemistry with a very calm demeanor, cut to the chase and dropped a bomb: "I will bet the university will be here after a large number of enterprises in this room are not."

"That was greeted with a hail of Wiffle balls," Faulkner recalled.

A year later, one of the summit organizers sent him a trophy of blue glass encasing a

◀◀ Waiting for the bats to take flight from under the Ann Richards Congress Avenue Bridge.

Photo by Erich Schlegel

◀ Students participate in a CPR class during the Dell Medical School 2018 summer camp at Gregory Gym on the University of Texas campus. The school's summer camp program aims to encourage youth to pursue careers in health fields.

Photo by Kelly West

silver-painted "platinum Wiffle ball" and a note: "Larry, you were right."

The 360 Summit lasted only three years, a casualty of the dot-com bust.

Opportunity Austin

The floor started to fall out from under the New Economy in early 2000 and a stock market plunge in March 2000 pushed many dot-com companies out of business.

"There was a lot of money chasing very little value and...it didn't create a healthy situation. It set the world up for the bust that happened. A lot of it was inflated and the air came out of it," said Faulkner, who served as UT president from 1998 to 2006.

The collapse of the dot-coms and the broader recession in 2001 hit Austin's high-tech industry hard and the fallout lingered for a long time.

"The national recession ended in November 2001, but it was not until two years later that Austin's high-tech employment started rising — six months after total national employment began to increase," according to a 2006 Dallas Fed report.

We were ill-prepared to bounce back from the downturn. The Greater Austin Chamber of Commerce had taken a hands-off approach to economic development for several years. Coming off the big, high-profile wins of yesteryear, they seemed comfortable to rest on their laurels. The Chamber also got distracted from its core mission by the "aquifer wars" and spent much of its time fighting local environmentalists at City Hall over specific real estate development projects instead of engaging in actual economic development.

"With the Austin economy roaring as it did for the past 20 or so years, it could be argued that there wasn't the need to aggressively retain and recruit firms. It was all Austin could do to contain the growth it had," consultant Market Street Services wrote in a 2003 analysis. "However, with the national and regional recessions continuing and no quick end in sight, Austin is not only faced with an urgent need to revitalize its economy but is forced to do so without the economic development infrastructure found in the majority of U.S. regions and states."

In addition, the Chamber of Commerce had been handling its own day-to-day operations poorly and was in dire financial condition, said Gary Farmer, president of Heritage Title, a respected business community leader and a Chamber of Commerce volunteer. For five years, he said, the Chamber's website had been "under construction."

That post-bust period "really showed us that we were not invincible, that we were mere mortals like everybody else in the world," Farmer said. "We better put our best foot forward and work at it if we really wanted to see a return."

In 2002, the Chamber hired a new CEO, Mike Rollins, an economic development pro then working in Nashville, to fix the organization. He immediately shifted the priority of the Chamber to a laser focus on, well, economic and business development.

▼ Pedal bike and rider

Photo by Ed Malcik

▶▶ JuiceLand offers nutrition with a touch of humor.

Photo by Noah Towery

The first step was to bring in a consultant, Market Street Services, to look at where Austin was, where it could go, and to lay out a blueprint for a regional business recruitment and retention strategy called Opportunity Austin.

Charles Barnett, a hospital executive and the new chairman of the Chamber board, tapped Farmer to lead Opportunity Austin. The Chamber was so strapped for cash that Farmer had to ask the Real Estate Council of Austin to pay for the consultants.

In an unprecedented effort, Farmer set out to raise $11 million from local businesses to implement this new way of doing business development in Central Texas.

"The business community decided to invest in the business of developing business, and they created this concept and this framework for how we would invest in getting businesses to come, grow or stay," said Laura Huffman, who oversaw the city's economic development efforts as an assistant city manager.

The city, led by Mayor Gus Garcia and City Manager Toby Futrell, chipped in $250,000 per year for Opportunity Austin's five-year plan. Austin Energy, our municipally owned utility, contributed as well by creating its own internal department aimed at recruiting clean energy companies to town. And Garcia formed a task force to craft an incentive policy based on the city's core values.

"Knowing our local community values and what the expectations were going to be, it was going to be up to (companies seeking incentives) to really quantify why Austin should accept their proposal," said Paul Saldaña, who served as Mayor Garcia's chief of staff.

At the end of five years, Opportunity Austin had shattered its goals by raising $14.3 million from investors, recruiting 143 companies, increasing wages by $3.8 billion and creating 123,000 jobs — about 50,000 more than planned.

By participating in Opportunity Austin, people and businesses were showing their pride in Austin and Central Texas. People responded. That's why it was so successful.

By the time the Great Recession hit in 2008, Austin was well positioned to weather the storm. Among the largest 100 metropolitan areas in the country, Austin was the last to fall into negative territory and the first to start growing again a year later.

And it hasn't stopped. The number of jobs in the Austin metro area grew more than 35 percent between 2008 and 2018, the largest percentage job gains of any other large area in the country and almost three times the national average, according to the Bureau of Labor Statistics.

Now on its fourth iteration, Opportunity Austin 4.0 is underway with Gary Farmer again leading the charge and a $25 million goal funded by the business community.

Austin Portrait: Mayor Gus Garcia

Photo by Casey Chapman Ross

Mayor Gus Garcia built bridges.

Not literally. He was an accountant by trade. But his true, incomparable talent was bringing people together.

Garcia fell ill and passed away in 2018 as I was working on this project so his voice is missing, but his life speaks volumes.

In 1972, he jumped into the center of political and social turmoil around school desegregation when he won a seat on the Austin Independent School District Board of Trustees. Garcia — together with another Austin legend, Wilhelmina Delco — fiercely advocated for the rights of minority children in Austin in the face of intense pressure. The two also helped to create Austin Community College in 1972 to provide greater access to higher education.

Education and creating opportunities for young people remained top priorities for Garcia throughout his life. In 2014, the school district opened the Gus Garcia Young Men's Leadership Academy in East Austin.

"If they were going to name a school for me I wanted it to be one with students that had challenges similar to me," Garcia told the ***Austin American-Statesman*** in 2016.

Garcia served on the Austin City Council for more than a decade, where he helped to mend wounds within the community and always looked for ways to make Austin more inclusive.

One of my fondest memories of my friend Gus, who I'd known and watched closely since the early 1980s, was a breakfast the two of us had at a great restaurant called El Sol y La Luna. I was considering running for mayor, and wanted — needed — the advice of this giant of Austin politics. Over migas, he scribbled a political map of Austin on the back of multiple napkins, drawing lines of connections between different people, disparate factions, key constituencies. It was an insightful, intuitive and passionate thesis on people, power, politics in Austin

— the good and the bad. He talked to me about the needs of the people in this community and my responsibility to serve them if I was to meet his expectations. And mine.

I'd give anything to have kept those napkins.

Gus served on the Council, mentored and continued to advise me during my time as mayor. In November 2001, he was elected mayor. He was mayor in the wake of the terrorist attacks of September 11, 2001, and the economic tumult of the dot-com bust. Given his extensive experience and steady, happy approach to things, he brought stability and a broad focus on economic opportunity for all.

"He tried not to focus so much on being the first Latino mayor, but at the same time I think he recognized the fact that he carried the burden of being the person to be able to speak to the experience of Mexican Americans or low-socioeconomic families and applying that to his role as the leader, as an influencer from a policy perspective," said Paul Saldaña, who served as Garcia's chief of staff.

Gus was a first many times, but that alone doesn't capture what made him special. He was someone who purposely put himself on the line over and over to show how things could be and should be done in Austin.

Chapter VIII: Expanding Opportunity

For those who are a part of it, the upside of the innovation economy is crystal clear. But it's much murkier to those on the outside.

As Austin has drawn people and businesses seeking to capitalize on some amazing economic opportunities, the simple market forces of supply and demand have driven up property values — and, correspondingly, property taxes and rents — particularly in neighborhoods close to downtown. And many longtime Austinites have trouble taking advantage of the opportunities that have brought the newcomers to town.

"A strong economy should not just be judged by how well corporations are doing, but it should be judged by how well working people are doing," said Cristina Tzintzún Ramirez, who co-founded the Workers Defense Project in Austin and served as its executive director from 2006 to 2015.

I absolutely believe that Austin can muster the necessary economic resources and political will to address our challenges head-on. But it isn't easy. It defies traditional or instinctive notions. It will take effort and a willingness to think differently. Simply talking about it or demanding a perfect outcome won't get us there. It won't work just to curse the growth that will come. Nor is it helpful to pretend that it's still 1980 and none of the growth and development has happened.

It will require a broad community effort, honest discussion and reflection and commitment from those at the forefront of this economy to help us address those challenges.

Divided Austin

Ours was a divided community long before Interstate Highway 35 cut Austin in two in the early 1960's. The racist 1928 master plan had forced African Americans to live in East Austin by restricting access to city services everywhere else while discriminatory deed restrictions and redlining had segregated Hispanic

◀◀ The city at night

Photo by Sean Mathis

◀ Sen. Kirk Watson joined Apple CEO Tim Cook, center, at the launch of an app development program with Austin Community College.

Photo by Catalin Abagui, courtesy of Austin Community College families to the same area. A city zoning plan pushed industrial facilities into East Austin as well.

The effects of those policies still lingered more than 60 years later when East Austin community leaders started to organize in the early 1990s to shut down the noxious industrial facilities that had been allowed to fester in their neighborhoods.

Paul Saldaña, who grew up in East Austin and worked for Mayor Gus Garcia, said there was a lot of mistrust and hard feelings from the minority communities in the neighborhood because it had taken city leaders so long to recognize the effects of the city's discriminatory past.

The community groups, such as PODER (People Organized in Defense of Earth and Her Resources), had done great work bringing attention to the issue and had scored some key wins over a petrochemical tank farm and the city-owned Holly Power Plant. As I mentioned earlier, I had been appointed by Governor Ann Richards as Chair of the Texas Air Control Board and had the chance to work directly with PODER on the tank farm issue. Out of this work, I created an environmental justice task force and placed a PODER leader in the chair.

For PODER and other community groups, changing the zoning that allowed the incompatible industrial uses amid residential neighborhoods was one of their top priorities.

When I became mayor in 1997, one of the first big decisions made by the City Council was to address the longstanding issue of incompatible uses in East Austin through zoning changes.

"From a broad perspective, they recognized that zoning changes were the most pragmatic way to make the Eastside more livable, healthy, and enjoyable for residents," Andrew Busch wrote in his book about the environmental history and racial injustice in Austin. "PODER drew on a recent report that found that new development in East Austin was stymied by mixed-used, interspersed residences and industries and irregular lots, all of which were 'freely' mixed for decades."

It worked. Probably too well.

While the zoning changes helped to improve the quality of life for the people living in the community, they also made the area much more appealing to newcomers looking for a place to live near downtown and Lady Bird Lake.

Pastor Joseph Parker, who led a planning process for the Chestnut neighborhood in the late 1990s, remembers that the area was home to a large number of undocumented immigrants as well as African-American seniors who had been renting for decades. There weren't sidewalks in the neighborhood nor were there parks or a grocery store or nearby health services, he said.

"While it was in the condition it was up until the '90s, they didn't want to live here," Parker said of the newcomers. "Once we started getting streets and sidewalks and other things like that, then they wanted to be here and they came. Now, we've got what we got."

We've seen it time and again that the efforts to improve the quality of life for current residents has had the effect of making an area more attractive to others.

▼ *For La Raza*, a restored mural outside the former Holly Power Plant, honors the Chicano heritage of the neighborhood.

Photo by Kelly West

▲ Holly Nguyen, 17, left, and Paola Juarez, 17, take notes during a microbiology lecture at the University of Texas at Austin campus. The high school students were participating in Dell Medical School's 2018 summer camp program, aimed at encouraging youth to pursue careers in health fields.

Photo by Kelly West

Mueller Municipal Airport, for example, was located in the middle of a residential community in East Austin. It was a source of constant complaints and residents wanted it gone — rightfully so. The airport finally moved in 1999 and the city redeveloped the site as a dense, pedestrian-friendly, mixed-income community with a large set-aside for affordable housing. Mueller has now become one of the most-desired neighborhoods in town, driving up property values and property taxes in the adjacent neighborhoods.

The Holly Street Power Plant, built in the early 1960s, was located on the banks of the Colorado River and right in the middle of a Latino neighborhood. Advocates urged its closing for years. Now that the plant has been decommissioned, it's being taken down piece by piece and new homes — expensive homes — started sprouting up as soon as the power plant shut down.

When Austin first really started to take off, we lacked policy tools that might have helped to stem the market forces that have driven the gentrification. That's changed somewhat over the past decade or so, and there is also strong commitment among political leaders and the public about the need to invest in affordable housing, as demonstrated by the recent approval of a $250 million bond initiative for affordable housing.

The resulting gentrification has changed East Austin, frustrating longtime residents who worked hard to improve the community. They deserve to be frustrated and unhappy. It's painful to work so hard to improve the quality of life for those who were treated unfairly and badly only to see others benefit from that work while those who should benefit are being displaced.

"There is another Austin that's not as satisfied about the prosperity," Parker said.

The market forces driving gentrification and displacement aren't unique to Austin. Our friends in Seattle, San Francisco, New York City and Washington, D.C., are struggling with similar issues. And it's evident that no one has yet cracked the code.

Even so, our greatest economic development asset today is our people — all of our people. And our biggest challenge is ensuring they all can participate and thrive in this ever-evolving economy.

The partnership between Merck and Huston-Tillotson University, a historically black university in East Austin, is a great example. Merck has worked with two HT professors to develop an undergraduate course in digital health for students in biology, computer science or mathematics. The company also offers paid internships for HT students to work on projects using health disparity data.

Apple CEO Tim Cook made a splash in 2017 when he came to town to launch an app development program with Austin Community College. That program offers affordable training that can get someone into the industry and open opportunity for folks who never thought that tech was for them.

Cook's visit was important to get the attention of other companies that have been resistant to putting the extra effort into training local people for the jobs they offer, said Mike Midgley, vice president of instruction at Austin Community College.

"We have to find a way for the native population that is here to participate in this, so it isn't an imported well-being," Midgley said.

Austin Community College has done great work adapting to fill our needs. For example, under legislation I co-authored in 2017, ACC was allowed to offer baccalaureate degrees in nursing, applied science and applied technology. The program provides working registered nurses an affordable and flexible opportunity to get a four-year degree, which gives them an economic leg up and addresses a huge workforce need. The first cohort of nursing students graduated in the summer of 2019.

We'll need more of these kinds of programs and we need to start thinking about how to do that.

We've been blessed to be able to cultivate an economy based on intellectual capital at the same time we've had great institutions of higher learning, including the premier University of Texas, in our midst. As we grow, the pipeline of educated workforce with degrees will need to increase and keep up with demand, but UT and Texas State University in San Marcos are essentially capped. We're going to need some place else to produce local talent.

▶ Young contestants at Rodeo Austin

Photo by Erich Schlegel

BORDEN
1461
BORDEN
1459
BORDEN
1472

Austin Portrait: The Rev. Joseph Parker, Jr.

Senior Pastor of David Chapel Missionary Baptist Church

Photo by Laura Skelding

The call to ministry started long before Joseph Parker, Jr., even started law school at the University of Texas at Austin. The son of a preacher in Birmingham, Ala., he sensed that the church was where he belonged, too, but was set on becoming a lawyer.

He preached his first sermon at David Chapel Missionary Baptist Church in 1982 during his last semester in law school and began seminary training while he worked as a trial lawyer with the Travis County Attorney.

"I was running both tracks," Pastor Parker said.

Pastor Parker was still practicing law — chief of litigation at the State Bar of Texas — when the longtime pastor of David Chapel passed away in 1992.

"I was clear at that point that God had called me to be the pastor," he said.

David Chapel has called Austin's Chestnut neighborhood home since 1926, two years before the city's 1928 master plan forced African Americans to live in East Austin. Many of today's congregants have deep roots in the neighborhood even though they're now scattered throughout the Austin area.

Pastor Parker has become a protector of the neighborhood and its longtime residents as the area has undergone significant changes. In 2000, he helped launch the Chestnut Neighborhood Revitalization Corp. to create affordable housing in the area through a community land trust and a project that serves low-income seniors. As chairman of the city's Citizens Bond Advisory Committee in 1998, Pastor Parker pressed for a small park in the neighborhood as well as sidewalks.

He has also contributed greatly to the larger community conversation about race, giving voice to history and present-day reality that often gets lost behind the story that Austin tells itself and others.

Pastor Parker has remained involved in the law, including teaching at the University of Texas School of Law. He has been honored by the Austin Bar Association and the State Bar of Texas for his leadership as a "trail blazer" for minority lawyers. In 2018, the Austin Bar Association named Pastor Parker the "Distinguished Lawyer of the Year."

▲ Ellsworth Kelly's "Austin" is part of the permanent collection at the Blanton Museum of Art on the University of Texas campus.

Photo by Ed Malcik

Austin Portrait: Cristina Tzintzún Ramirez, Founder of Jolt

▲ Protesting outside the Texas Capitol

Photo by Julia Shumlin, courtesy of Jolt

Cristina Tzintzún Ramirez was still an undergrad at The University of Texas at Austin when she co-founded the Workers Defense Project in 2006 to help low-income workers organize for fair working conditions.

"In some ways it was good I was young because I was a bit naive about what I was biting off," she says now. "I had no idea what I was doing. I was totally unqualified. I didn't even have a car; I rode a bicycle everywhere. But that organization evolved from an idea, an idea about how our economy should work and who it should benefit."

The goal of the Workers Defense Project was bigger than just improving and guaranteeing basic legal rights, Tzintzún said, but also trying to ensure the workers and their labors be given the value and dignity they deserve.

Over a decade, she helped to build up the worker-centered organization to become a major voice at Austin City Hall. Workers Defense Project pushed the City Council to pass ordinances to improve safety at construction sites and require companies that receive city incentives or build city projects to abide by certain safety and wage standards. In 2014, the policy director at the Workers Defense Project, Gregorio Casar, was elected to the City Council.

While at Workers Defense, she developed an electoral program. Many of the organization's members were undocumented and couldn't vote, but they had family members who were eligible to vote. That work gave rise to her next project: Jolt.

"I wanted to form Jolt to really harness the power and voice and votes of the Latino community," said Tzintzún, who noted that more than 2 million Latinos will turn 18 over the next decade and 95 percent of them are U.S. citizens. "We're called Jolt because when Latinos come out and vote, we intend to be a shock to the political system, not just of our state but the entire country."

Launched shortly after the 2016 election, Jolt caught the eye of many in 2017 with a protest on the steps of the Texas Capitol that featured young Latinas in their "sparkly, ruffled" Quinceañera dresses. The protest of Senate Bill 4, which targeted the immigrant community, reached an estimated 50 million people, Tzintzún said.

Now the focus is on getting young Latinx to organize in their own communities and on college campuses in the run-up to the 2020 election and beyond.

In the summer of 2019, Tzintzún resigned from Jolt to jump into the Democratic Primary for U.S. Senate. The election is in 2020.

◀ Cristina Tzintzún Ramirez

Photo by Kelly West

Chapter IX: A Model Healthy Community

OUR LITTLE COLLEGE TOWN HAD GROWN UP FAST AND STRONG, BUT A CRITICAL PIECE OF BIG-CITY INFRASTRUCTURE WAS MISSING: A MEDICAL SCHOOL.

The voters of Texas had split their ticket back in 1881, sending the University of Texas Medical Branch to the trade center of Galveston while planting the flagship university campus in the Capital City of Austin. As former University of Texas Chancellor Francisco Cigarroa put it, the two institutions "were separated at birth."

More than a century later, Austin was one of the largest cities in the country without a medical school and not having a medical school made the University of Texas at Austin an outlier among the Tier One research institutions.

For our community, the absence of a medical school meant that folks were missing out on some cutting-edge medical treatment and cures. People were forced to travel to other cities for care, and many — particularly if they were uninsured or economically disadvantaged— had to wait far too long to get the care they needed. We needed more doctors, and other communities had demonstrated that a good way to get doctors to serve the community was to grow them locally.

For our economy, we'd never get a real economic foothold in biotech, health sciences and medical research without serious academic medicine. Folks in the business community understood that if we made a wise investment in medical education and research, we would dramatically enlarge the scope of our knowledge-based economy. Austin would suddenly be running in a race for discovery and healing that stretches from Houston to Hong Kong. The Chamber of Commerce had considered a medical school a priority for years and labeled it a "breakthrough idea."

There had been efforts to get UT a medical school since at least the 1950s with visionary leaders like Frank Denius arguing its value. Notable physician Dr. Ken Shine became the Executive Vice Chancellor for Health at the University of Texas System in 2003, and he quickly began the push for a medical school at UT-Austin.

And there were times we thought we saw a path, including maybe partnering with the University of Texas Medical Branch in Galveston, the state's very first medical school. Unfortunately, Hurricane Ike hit

◀◀ Vista from the Dell Medical School

Photo by Albert Vecerka courtesy of Esto and Page

▼ At the park

Photo by John Langmore

Galveston Island in 2008 and did great damage to the school. It also washed away the possibility of UT-Austin being able to affiliate with UTMB in a comprehensive, meaningful way.

By 2011, Dr. Shine and some folks in key positions determined the time was ripe for another full-on effort at getting a medical school in Austin. They asked me — sometimes very insistently — to lead the effort.

▼ UT tower at night

Photo by Sean Mathis

10 Goals in 10 Years

As a cancer survivor myself, I'm pretty passionate about healthcare and access to care, and I'd been involved in the discussions about a medical school and other health-related matters for over a decade.

I'd talked to a lot of people about our needs, and it was very clear that those needs were bigger than just a medical school. We crafted a vision that encompassed a broad set of goals with an eye toward ensuring the whole community would benefit. It would be a roadmap toward better health and a healthier economy.

I wanted this vision to be a catalyst for our great institutions and great thinkers and great hearts to come together and create something bigger than they could ever do alone. And it was going to take some time. After a lot of discussion and deliberation, I boiled it down to 10 Goals that we wanted — that we needed — to achieve in 10 Years:

1. Build a medical school
2. Build a modern teaching hospital
3. Establish modern, uniquely Austin health clinics in our neighborhoods
4. Develop laboratories and other facilities for public and private research
5. Launch a new commercialization incubator
6. Make Austin a center for comprehensive cancer care
7. Provide needed psychiatric care and facilities
8. Improve basic infrastructure, and create a sense of place
9. Bolster the medical examiner's office
10. Solve the funding puzzle

Each of these individual pieces fit together to achieve the big vision.

For example, the city's old Brackenridge Hospital, which was later called University Medical Center at Brackenridge, had served as a teaching hospital for over a half century. The change in name had been, in part, to highlight the medical residency program at Brack and claim some medical education in Austin. But the hospital, which also served as our community's safety net hospital, hadn't been designed as a 21st century teaching hospital and it hadn't received a significant upgrade in decades. While the care was excellent and it was the region's only Level I trauma center, we needed a new teaching and safety-net hospital if we were going to have a medical school.

We also needed more clinics where doctors could train and, importantly, our people could receive care. We wanted the clinics to be "uniquely Austin", meaning they might do things differently in assuring the health of our people. And they needed to be in places that made care easier for the underserved and poor.

There was also a clear need for improved cancer and psychiatric care while the economic engine could use additional research labs and increased commercialization infrastructure. And the medical examiner's office needed new digs, morbid as it sounds.

▼ Giselle Dancers Ashley Lynn Sherman & James Fuller

Photo by Anne Marie Bloodgood

We didn't know if all these goals could be achieved in one place, but we knew the most transformative opportunity was to anchor many of them in one location and for that we had a goal of ensuring the necessary infrastructure and creating a sense of place. Finally, we had to figure out how to fund it all.

In September 2011, I gave a speech laying out the 10 Goals in 10 Years. At that point, the goals were just that — GOALS. We didn't have answers to most of the questions. We needed to get more brains working on how to reach these shared goals. Every big vision needs a thousand mothers.

Everybody wanted to know how we were going to pay for it, and we didn't have answers yet. I had to repeatedly urge folks not to jump to conclusions because we were still working through our needs, analyzing possibilities, evaluating what was practical and then we'd figure out the funding. The straightforward approach of asking the Texas Legislature for funding simply wasn't politically feasible. So, we focused on coming up with a new playbook.

The final funding plan included a big, negotiated commitment from the University of Texas System to pay for the buildings and specific funding for the operation of the school that included seed money to recruit top faculty.

Our safety net and teaching hospital had been under the management of what is today called Ascension Seton since 1995 when the City of Austin essentially created a public/private partnership with Seton. In 2004, Travis County voters created a healthcare district known as Central Health and the district stepped into the City's shoes as the public partner. Seton, through its mothership Ascencion Health, agreed to build a modern facility without any taxpayer dollars.

But we were still missing a piece of the funding puzzle. The agreement with the University of Texas System required us to find another $35 milllion a year. We concluded that our best source for that revenue was asking the voters of Travis County to support a property tax increase that would help to support the medical school.

Going to the voters was a huge risk. But we had the benefit of a lot of community buy-in because the big vision — rather than just a single project — did have a thousand mothers and appealed to a broad array of constituencies.

The voters of Travis County embraced the vision and, in November 2012, approved the property tax increase for Central Health, our countywide healthcare district, to invest in our health and future. Our people were willing to listen, plan for their future and invest in it.

◄◄ The lay of the land

Photo by Sean Mathis

▼ Daybreak

Photo by John Langmore

Creating Health

Because of the unique local tax investment in Dell Medical School, the school has a strong focus on and interest in the community, particularly folks who are uninsured or underserved by the healthcare system.

"In our DNA is our connection to our community and so ultimately the research and education mission really ought to be disciplined around what the community needs," said Dr. Clay Johnston, the inaugural dean of Dell Med.

He recruited world-class faculty members who began to improve our system of healthcare delivery even before the school welcomed its first class of students in 2016.

"We have an obligation to help lead, at least in the ideas and programs that can address those needs," Dr. Johnston added. "We won't meet all those needs; it's too big. But if we can get the systems of care working better so those needs are delivered on, that would be great, and it is part of our role."

Dell Med has partnered with Central Health — the public healthcare district that levies the property tax supporting the medical school — and the operator of our safety-net and teaching hospital, Ascension Seton. The task of that collaboration is nothing short of rethinking the entire healthcare delivery system.

"It is really about creating health," said Dr. Mark Hernandez, chief medical officer of the collaboration.

The Dell Seton Medical Center at the University of Texas, which opened across the street from the medical school in 2017, provides a state-of-the-art teaching hospital for students and residents as well as top-flight care for patients, regardless of their ability to pay. Since 2012, the number of medical residents providing care in Travis County has increased 30 percent.

As Dell Med develops the system innovations to improve health while decreasing costs, it has an array of laboratories to test the ideas, including the hospital, the clinics in the medical school's Health Transformation Building and the other "uniquely Austin" community health clinics, including the Sandra Joy Anderson Community Health and Wellness Center at Huston-Tillotson University and the Southeast Health and Wellness Center.

For example, Dr. Amy Young and her colleagues in Dell Med's Department of Women's Health, have worked with Seton to develop a new drug protocol that has reduced opioid prescriptions for new moms by 40 percent. This extraordinary work is already improving health in our community.

▼▶ A sculpture of blues legend Stevie Ray Vaughan stands on the south shore of Lady Bird Lake.

Photos by Sean Mathis

The wait for a clinic patient to see a joint specialist has been reduced from a year to two weeks due to a Dell Med project. The LiveStrong Cancer Institutes of the Dell Medical School are rethinking the entire continuum of cancer care with a patient-centered focus. And the Department of Population Health — one of the first in the country — is taking responsibility for the health of the people of Travis County — all of the people of Travis County. They're looking at new technologies and new ways of using data to help people get healthy when they're sick – and new strategies and partnerships to help them stay healthy when they're well.

Rethinking Brain Health

Mental illness is common. Often hidden but common. And brain health, in concept, is no different than heart health. It should be integrated in the healthcare system for the rest of the body. Yet we deal with it differently — and poorly at that.

For the most part, what we have is a public system that primarily helps people in crisis, either in emergency rooms or jails — the most expensive and ineffective places to provide care. The result is less than half of people with psychiatric conditions receive effective treatment.

What we're missing is preventative care that helps day to day. Care necessary to keep folks out of crisis.

The 10 Goals in 10 Years included some pretty ambitious plans for improving that system. We made some great progress in the early years, such as opening a psychiatric emergency department and the Judge Guy Herman Center for Mental Health Crisis Care. Integral Care, our local mental health authority, created mobile outreach teams and bolstered training for first responders and others in the community.

But I saw an unexpected opportunity to do much, much more when a 2014 state report concluded that five of Texas' 10 state psychiatric hospitals were essentially unsalvageable and had to be replaced. The Austin State Hospital, parts of which date back to the 1850s, was one of the worst.

As state leaders started discussing what to do with those hospitals, I asked the folks at Dell Med to offer up some ideas to do more than just rebuild the building. They said we should redesign the entire system of brain healthcare.

The phrase "brain health" is an integral part of the redesign. We've been very intentional in using that language because brain health appropriately expresses it as

▶▶ Leap of faith during SXSW

Photo by Ed Malcik

the medical condition it is. And "brain health" doesn't have the stigma that "mental health" often sadly carries.

In 2017, the Texas Legislature put a down payment toward replacing the crumbling state hospitals and the Dell Medical School was tapped to lead the redesign of the Austin State Hospital. Dr. Steve Strakowski, Dell Med's Associate Vice President for Regional Mental Health, is spearheading that effort. Our initial goal has evolved into something much, much bigger: a 21st century brain health continuum of care that provides folks the right care at the time in a person-centered way, regardless of their ability to pay.

The Legislature continued its investment in the redesign of the Austin State Hospital and the brain health continuum of care with a $165 million appropriation to construct the first phase of the replacement hospital. The target date for occupancy and operation is 2023. I'm pleased we also passed legislation to consider how the Dell Medical School might enhance the governance of ASH.

In our vision, the ASH Campus will be to brain health what the Cleveland Clinic is to heart health or MD Anderson is to cancer care. It will be a leader in neuropsychiatric research, the development of new clinical treatments and modeling integrated care services across a continuum of providers, services and intensities.

Health and Economic Growth

Before Dell Med, Austin didn't have a chance at recruiting or building up businesses in the life sciences sector, said Gary Farmer, who spearheads much of our community's economic development outreach through Opportunity Austin. Now, it's a different story.

"We're brand new, we're pretty small so why would companies listen? It's because we've aggregated these people who are really about transforming the health system and we're focused on different business concepts as well to open up new opportunities," Dean Johnston said.

That Merck chose to come to Austin — and embrace our big vision — when Dell Med is still in its infancy speaks volumes about the economic potential.

Capital City Innovation, a non-profit entity that launched in 2017, is tasked with harnessing that potential to create an Innovation Zone that will run from the medical school and teaching hospital complex to the river. The goal is to develop a place of creative energy that grows entrepreneurs and thinkers using the medical school as a catalyst and fosters both inclusive healthcare and inclusive economic growth.

If any place is going to revolutionize healthcare, it's Austin, said Christopher Laing, executive director of Capital City Innovation. We've got a strong academic landscape, an entrepreneurial culture, a robust corporate presence and community organizations that are interested in bolstering the health and social safety net.

"We have the exact right ingredients here in Austin for the future of healthcare," Laing said.

Dell Med is also focused on seeking out the good ideas from folks that are already here and helping them to nurture those ideas through several different initiatives, including Texas Health Catalyst and the Texas Health CoLab.

"We're actively seeking (innovation) out in the community, finding it, supporting it, collaborating with those folks and pushing it forward," said Dr. Mini Kahlon, vice dean of the health ecosystem for Dell Med. "Really, being the gear shift under all these other really fantastic efforts."

Austin Community College is playing significant role in fostering new ideas, as well, with the creation of the ACC Bioscience Incubator, which offers wet lab space for biotech start-ups as well as amazing learning opportunities for the students. One of its early start-ups won the $100,000 top prize from the MassChallenge Texas in 2018. ACC is the only community college in Texas with wet lab space.

"We want to help the regional economy by having the wet lab space, but we absolutely want it to tie back to helping our students," said Mike Midgley, ACC's vice president of instruction.

Austin Community College has made it a priority to provide affordable access to the training needed to take advantage of the opportunity created by growing healthcare industry, including a new mid-career program to help working nurses get a bachelor's degree.

And Dell Med is reaching out to younger students through partnerships with local school districts and the Health Sciences Summer Camp where middle school and high school students get a hands-on introduction to the health professions by Dell Med's faculty and students.

All of these efforts are intended to work toward the twin goals of becoming a model healthy community with an economic engine that drives opportunity far and wide — to all Austinites.

RULES
blu
blu
blu
blu

Austin Portrait: Dr. Mark Hernandez

chief medical officer, Community Care Collaborative

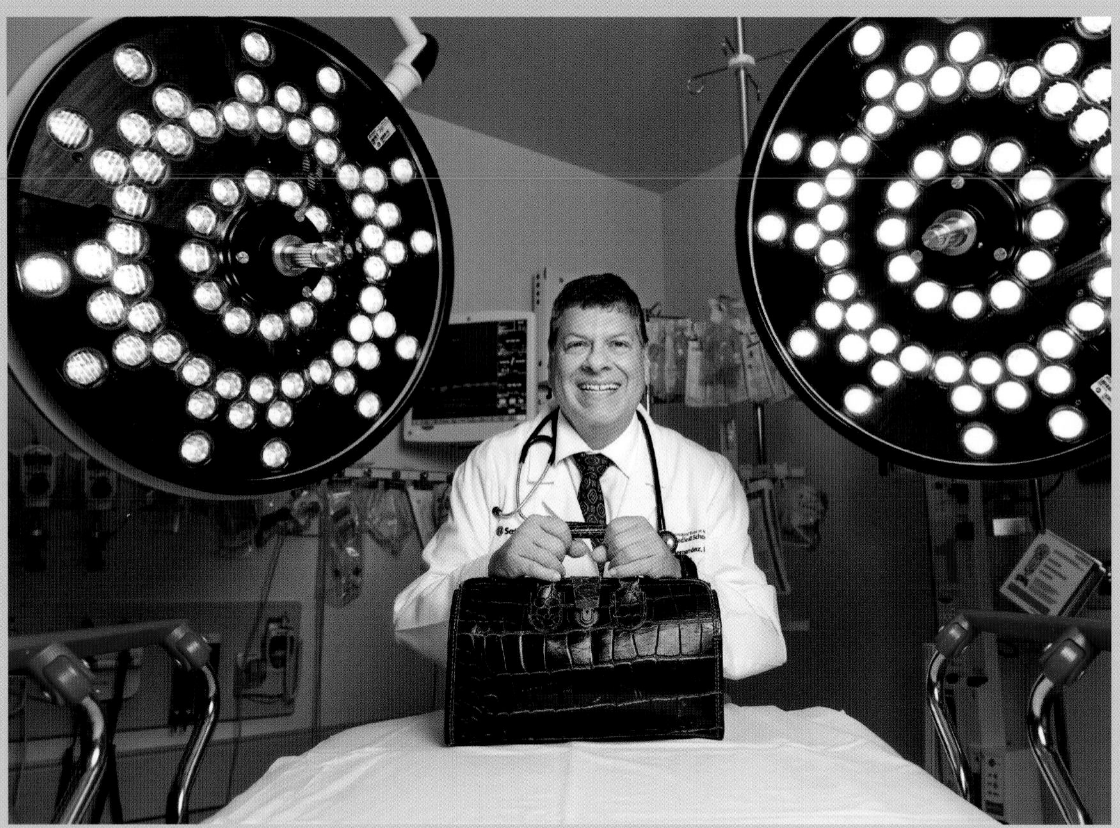

▲ Photo by Laura Skelding

Providing care to people in need has been a constant for Dr. Mark Hernandez, first as an intensive-care nurse at a public hospital in Houston and then as a doctor at the safety-net hospital in Austin.

Now, he's responsible for the health and well-being of more than 100,000 Travis County residents in his role as chief medical officer overseeing the partnership between the local public healthcare district and Ascension Seton, which operates our safety-net hospital.

His job is to transform our local healthcare delivery system for residents who are low-income and uninsured so that it's focused on "creating health" rather than simply treating illness. It's a mammoth undertaking that he's tackling along with many leading health professionals at the Dell Medical School, Dell Seton Medical Center, community providers and others.

"I firmly believe that healthcare — and not just healthcare but high-quality healthcare — is a right of every person in this country, documented or not," Dr. Hernandez said. "If you are here and you are ailing, we should help you. If you are here and you are not ailing, we should keep you there and not let you become sick. We can do it. It is possible."

And ensuring that people are treated with dignity and respect in that system is essential, he said. They need to feel cared for and believe that their healthcare providers are there to help them.

Dr. Hernandez has had his own experience being on the receiving-end of care when he suffered a heart attack at age 32 during his first year of medical school.

"I got to see way more of healthcare in my first year of medical school than I ever would have thought," Dr. Hernandez said. "It has not been lost on me that I am the product of a healthcare system that worked for me."

"The way the system works for me is the way that system should work for everybody," he added.

Austin Portrait: Dr. Mini Kahlon

Vice Dean of the Health Ecosystem at Dell Medical School

▼ Photo by Kelly West

Dr. Mini Kahlon, a neuroscientist by training, had worked at start-ups before but not like this one.

On Day Zero, the Dell Medical School was a $100 million operation at a Tier One research university with a heavily diversified line of business and a white-hot spotlight. And yet, few of the other necessary elements — such as the people — were there to make it real, she said.

"No one could have guessed what it meant to start up an enterprise like this," said Dr. Kahlon, who was "faculty #4 or something" at Dell Med and serves as the vice dean of the health ecosystem.

Dr. Kahlon was leading the innovation arm of the University of California San Francisco when Dell Med's inaugural Dean Clay Johnston lured her to his new venture in Austin. Previously, she'd had experience in the start-up world, though it didn't "feed her soul," which led her back to science and UCSF.

She didn't know much about Austin beyond SXSW but has been intrigued by the "prototyping culture" that permeates much of Austin.

Dr. Kahlon points to a time maybe a month after arriving in Austin where she was with her family downtown and they ran across this small gathering of specialty food trucks where there was beer and music and someone had thrown hula hoops on the sidewalk that her daughter picked up and enjoyed.

"That was the moment I remember just looking at my husband and saying 'this is kind of awesome.' And it's not just those pieces but the fact that that it had just come together as 'let's try this out.' It's part of a prototyping culture, a culture that just riffs on stuff, tries things out," Dr. Kahlon said.

Dr. Kahlon said Austin feels like a "21st-century frontier town" that's full of adrenaline and drive and is a little chaotic. There's no fear of the next big idea or the big concept, she said.

"There's always this sense of 'yeah, we can try that,'" she said.

She believes it"s a once-in-a-lifetime opportunity for building something significant from scratch that will create real change for a lot of people.

"I feel like I'm suddenly awake," Dr. Kahlon said.

Chapter X: Great Days, Great Ideas, Great Future

Isn't it a great day to be in Austin, Texas? For over 20 years, I've asked that question at the beginning of lots and lots speeches I've given to all sorts of crowds. It gets the same enthusiastic, positive reaction every time. Because the answer is that it's almost always a great day if you're in Austin, Texas.

There really is something special about Austin. It's changed. No question. But the people, the environment, the spirit and the character that attracted people through the decades and caused folks to stay are still attracting people. And the people still find good reason to stay.

We have a responsibility and a need to preserve those qualities.

Through a lot of trial and error over the years, I've developed a set a ground rules that have helped me face the challenges of our community. As I've shared my ground rules at countless graduations and other events, others seem to have found them pretty helpful, too. And I think they might be helpful to others as we confront the opportunities and, yes, the challenges of tomorrow.

Here are a few of my ground rules:

Be biased toward action: Channel creativity and passion into a bias toward acting and getting things done. Fear of failure has to be set aside and turned upside down. Experimenting with new approaches is part of creativity. They may not turn out exactly as predicted or hoped. But we need to try, learn from the experiment and act.

Likewise, we can't be paralyzed and not act for fear that some better idea or better deal might come along down the road. Many of our challenges are time sensitive. Action is needed now. We want to be thoughtful, but we can't afford to be still. Sitting around wishing and thinking and hoping a better idea will pop up can exacerbate the challenges.

Throw away the labels: Politics and policy today is being hurt by labels. People label each other and then stop learning from or listening to others because the label is shorthand for all they need or want to know about them. We lose out on ideas when we do that. Usually, there's more to a person (and what they think) than some label.

◄◄ UT Tower
Photo by Erich Schlegel

▼ Game Day
Photo by Erich Schlegel

Speak plainly and listen carefully: Big decisions require people to understand what they're dealing with. That can't be done if folks are vague in how they communicate. The goals and consequences of acting or not acting need to be clearly stated. And we need to be sure we're hearing what people are saying about how they feel. Too often, the rhetoric and adversarial debate masks what people are trying to tell us. It's importand to listen and always look for new means or methods to hear each other.

The "84% Rule": Austin sometimes defines "consensus" as 100% agreement, which slows processes and many times leads to nothing happening at all. After all, if you have to have everyone (or nearly everyone agreeing) you could easily end up with something that's not workable or you make someone or some group too powerful because they can essentially veto something the majority would like. The truth is you generally can't meet everyone's concept of perfection. There will always be nitpickers, naysayers and know-it-alls. We need to listen carefully to points of view, but then move, even though some won't see it as perfect.

I follow what I've come to call the "84% Rule" If you can get a large part of your constituency to say they'll go along with something even though it's not perfect or the way they might do it, take it and run. Why 84%? Well, that was my margine for re-election as mayor. That's the joke. Of course, it doesn't have to be 84%, but it makes the point. You're not going to satisfy everyone.

By the way, if you accept that you're not going to meet everyone's concept of perfection but will still try to make progress, don't demand your concept of perfection either. Pray you get 84% of what you want.

Create new and different constituencies (and don't create unnecessary enemies): Approach every challenge, opportunity, program or project with the goal of growing or creating new and different constituencies. Progress will be best achieved if we step back from our laser focus on a solution and ask if there are changes, modifications or tweaks that still achieve the goal we seek and also bring others to the table with support. It ought to go without saying, but in this day and age, I guess we need to say it over and over again: Don't create unnecessary enemies. You may need those people the next time. Getting what you want doesn't mean you have to destroy those who disagree.

Have a short-term focus with a long-term vision: If you had asked me the week before I was told I had cancer in my early 30's what I thought I'd be doing 15 or 20 years from then, I could have told you what I planned things to be like. I thought I had the world by the tail. At

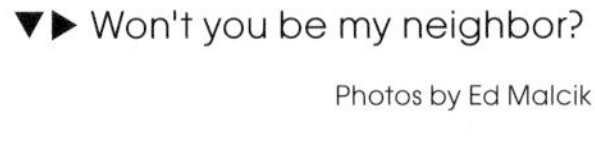
▼▶ Won't you be my neighbor?

Photos by Ed Malcik

first, even being told I was sick and dealing with surgeries and chemo didn't really change my approach that much. But finding a new tumor related to the original cancer on a routine CT scan a couple of years later prompted a little more introspection. I started living my life more in increments of time where I would focus on what's in front of me with an urgency to achieve it now. The best laid plans may not be there. In other words, I think we ought to have a short-term focus. Get things done while you can. Of course, do those things with the hope that we'll have a good, long run and that they will fit into a long-term vision of good.

As part of living this way, I think it's very important for us to routinely reassess our core values and assets. Some folks will say, "Your values shouldn't change". But, they do. Life happens and that changes things. It might be happy changes (I think of my young granddaughter) or things that hurt (like getting sick). It also is the kind of thing a community needs to do. Elections ought to be helpful in this regard. But assessing values and assets has to be done not in a political sense of who might be winning and losing, up or down. It can't be done in a purely nostalgic sense either. Protecting what's core is important and necessary. Recognizing new assets and advancing them is also a key to a focus and a vision. A willingness to admit weaknesses, including those that may have developed or grown because of strongly held positions of the past, is a must.

Lather, rinse and repeat: Process matters. Process should complement and enhance the outcome. It should not itself become the ultimate goal and impede getting to the outcome.

Process should be orderly, without jumping to the conclusions we want or we think we already know. I suggest people start the process by coming to some agreement on the purpose behind what they're considering: Why are they doing this? Why do people feel so strongly abou the issue? Then, explore the possibilities. Wave magic wands and explore all the possibilities based upon the purpose to be achieved. After that, though, honestly explore the practicalities of those possibilities. From that reduction, create the plan, including how it will be led and how it can be changed along the way. And of course, all along, ask who ought to be involved.

Then repeat. The plan ought to assure follow-through. As big ideas become something real, they need to be nurtured and tended. They require regular maintenance. Maybe lathering up more than once to get everything done.

Hope matters: Never forget that hope matters. Hope is what motivates people. Hope is what prompts someone to work to protect something special about our

home or create something new that will enhance our quality of life. We need to ask ourselves as we make every decision: Are we creating hope, being hopeful, focusing on the positive of what we can be?

Austin was built on hope. It has evolved over a century and a half from a tiny frontier capital to the Live Music Capital of the World to a focal point in a worldwide information and knowledge economy because Austin has always been ready for the new idea.

The idea that it's not only important but necessary to protect the beauty and environment.

The idea that we should shed the sins of the past and embrace all of the community and the value everyone adds.

The idea that passion for a place can make it the best of itself.

The idea that tomorrow belongs to Austin.

▲ Improv poetry on the streets of downtown

Photo by Ed Malcik

TRINITY
JACKALOPE
SXSW
POEMS
Improv
Poetry

Photojournal: Austin Unlimited

"Your Essential Magnificence", by James Talbot. City of Austin Art in Public Places Collection
Photo by Noah Towery

ASK ABOUT MY
LARGE
HADRON COLLIDER
SLEEP
LOST DOG
NO PARKIN
AUSTIN
MOTEL

South Congress
Photos by Noah Towery

▲ The Austin Symphony Orchestra

Photo by Tyler Schmitt

▲ Ballet Austin performance of *The Nutcracker*, Choreography: Stephen Mills, Dancer-Courtney Holland.

Photo by Anne Marie Bloodgood

▲ Waiting to cross South Congress

Photos by Noah Towery

▲ The Texas heat gets to all of us at one point

Photos by Noah Towery

BIKE
LANE
CLOSED
SHARE
THE
ROAD

Awesome Mural

Photo by Ed Malcik

ORDER HERE

◀▲ Ice cream shop on South Congress and the bats coming out at night

Photos by Noah Towery

Loyalty
Honor

▲ Mural in East Austin

Photo by Ed Malcik

▲ Waller Creek runs through the east side of downtown and is undergoing a major restoration.

Photos by Sean Mathis

▲ Cooling off.

Photos by Sean Mathis

◀ Just outside the city limits

Photos by Sean Mathis

Austin Raceway

Photo courtesy of COTA

Austin Raceway

Photo courtesy of COTA

YAMAHA
Eurasian Bank
movistar
99
SEMAKIN DIDEPAN
YAMAHA
Eurasian Bank
JORGELORENZO99
ENEOS
YAMALUBE
SECTOR
YAMAHA

▲◀ Rodeo

Photos by Erich Schlegel

1 Figura

Raquel's Party Land on East Cesar Chavez Street

Photo by Noah Towery

E WILL ASSIST YOU
DO NOT TOUCH BOOTS

◀ Inside Heritage Boot Co.

▲ Austin yard bird

Photos by Noah Towery

▲ Eeyore's Birthday

Photo by Ed Malcik

▲ Eeyore's Birthday

Photo by John Langmore

COSTILLAS
COSTILLAS DE
CHULETAS DE
CHUK
Budweiser

◀◀ Taqueria leftovers.

Photo by John Langmore

▲ Meaty meat.

Photo by Erich Schlagel

Laguna Gloria Park

Photos by Noah Towery

In Bloom

Photo by Noah Towery

◀◀ Wangechi Mutu, "Water Woman," 2017. Artwork © Wangechi Mutu. Courtesy of The Contemporary Austin - Laguna Gloria

Photos by Noah Towery

▲ Tom Friedman, "Looking Up," 2015. Artwork © Tom Friedman. Courtesy of The Contemporary Austin - Laguna Gloria
▶ Steps on path through Laguna Gloria

Photos by Noah Towery

09

East Austin Home with Cat

photo by John Langmore

▲ Construction never stops these days, and a view of the capitol at sundown.

Photos by Ed Malcik

STOP
ALL WAY

BEVO XIV

◀▲ UT Football and Bevo.
Photos by Erich Schlegel

▲ Saltillo Project Construction

photos by Ed Malcik

Panoramic view of Austin

Photo by Sean Mathis

ESPRESSO
CHAMPAGNE
CHAIN LUBE

Photos by Noah Towery

▲▶ Skyline

Photos by Sean Mathis

183
EXCEPT BICYCLES
ONLY

Mr.Catfish
The
Best
Catfish
In
Town!!
SMOKED·GRILLED·GLAZED
ALLIGATOR
ON-A-STICK
DO NOT
ENTER
BLOOMING
ONION
POPCORN
SHRIMP & FRIES
Mr. Catfish & More
TOWING/BOOTING
ENFORCED
AUTHORIZED PAID PARKING ONLY
24 HOURS A DAY 7 DAYS A WEEK
TX TOWING 512-412-5367
FOR TOWED VEHICLES CALL
HOT
FRESH
MINI
DONUTS
ICE CREAM
BLOOMING
ONION
RIBBON
FRIES

◀◀ SXSW

Photo by Ed Malcik

▲ SXSW

Photo by Erich Schlegel

◀ SXSW

Photo by Ed Malcik

Photos by Noah Towery

KEEP
LUCY IN DISGUISE
with Diamonds
IMAGINE...
ASHBURY
HAIGHT
78704

▶ Nightlife: Cyclist and food Truck

Photos by Sean Mathis

▶▶ Refreshments

Photo by Noah Towery

Pizza B
Slice

DOS EQUIS
RAY PRIM
LIVE AT
THE CONTINENTAL
James
McMurtry
Wed @ Midnite
GOAT

▲▶ Sights on 6th street

Photo by Noah Towery

MAMA
Casino
El Camino
OPEN

Grafitti Mural

Photo by John Langmore

Live Music at the Continental Club

Photos by Noah Towery

FENDER

Evening food hustle

Photos by John Langmore

PICADILLO
BEAN & CHEESE

▲ Lake Austin with downtown in the distance

Photo by Sean Mathis

▲ Rodeo Austin

Photos by Erich Schlegel

BULLET PROOF
JIM BEAM
BULLET PROOF
COMMITTEE
2010
Justin
BOOTS

Buffalo Soldiers reenactors at Austin Rodeo

Photos by Erich Schlegel

▲ Church scene

Photo by John Langmore

▲ The Lost Well Bar

Photo by Ed Malcik

▲ Goat gone AWOL

photo by Ed Malcik

▲ No need to fear the giant armadillo

photo by Ed Malcik

The Joe R. and Teresa Lozano Long Center for the Performing Arts

◀ Photos by Erich Schlegel

▲ Photo by Gary Ross

▲ Life in Austin

Photos by John Langmore

▲ Fly fishing in Lady Bird Lake

Photo by Erich Schlegel

▲ Good boy

Photo by Sean Mathis

EXIT

▲ Local music always greets visitors at Austin-Bergstrom International Airport

photo by Tim Griffith, courtesy of Page

▲ Antone's has moved over the years but its dedication to the blues has remained unchanged.

Photos by Casey Chapman Ross

▲ Inside the Capitol

Photos by Casey Chapman Ross

▲ State bird

Photo by Noah Towery

▶ Texas sky

Photo by Erich Schlegel

SOUTH AUSTIN EXPRESS

Profiles in Excellence

Biographies of the organizations whose generous support of this work made it possible. Listed alphabetically below, they appear in the book in the order in which the companies were founded in Austin.

Austin Chambers of Commerce

Connecting Knowledge, Power, Passion, and Values

IN 1952, AS AUSTIN WAS BECOMING ESTABLISHED AS ONE OF TEXAS' MAJOR METROPOLITAN AREAS, THE MERGER OF TILLOTSON COLLEGE AND SAMUEL HUSTON COLLEGE CREATED HUSTON-TILLOTSON COLLEGE. BOTH SCHOOLS HAD BEEN FOUNDED IN AUSTIN IN THE 1870S DURING THE POST-CIVIL WAR ERA TO educate freed slaves and their descendants. The city of Austin's first institution of higher learning and only Historically Black College and University, the school became Huston–Tillotson University (HT) in 2005.

Huston-Tillotson University today boasts a diverse population of students from around the world. HT has been a long-time trail blazer in the community and a jewel in the violet crown of Austin.

While its roots go back close to a century-and-a-half, Huston-Tillotson University has an extraordinary history and an incredible future reflected in the University's vision: A connected world where diversity of thought matters. HT embraces its 21st Century mission of nurturing a legacy of leadership and excellence in education, connecting knowledge, power, passion, and values.

A Leader in Education

The University is a historic institution with its faith-based roots firmly planted in the United Methodist Church and United Church of Christ. The president serves as the chief executive officer of the university.

HT's 24-acre campus near Interstate 35 in downtown Austin is located on Bluebonnet Hill. From that center of learning, the University provides opportunities to a diverse population for academic achievement with an emphasis on academic excellence, spiritual and ethical development, entrepreneurship, civic engagement, and leadership in a nurturing environment. On campus there is a noticeable sense of a strong family environment with a shared goal of student success.

As a liberal arts institution, Huston-Tillotson University is accredited by the Southern Association of Colleges and Schools Commission on Colleges. The University awards undergraduate four-year degrees in business, education, humanities, natural sciences, social sciences, science, and technology. A multi-cultural, multi-ethnic, and multi-faith institution, the University is committed to education as the great equalizer for all. There is a common belief on campus in the power of possibility striking the perfect balance of honoring our history while forging boldly into the future.

creating engaged citizens committed to creating a beloved community for all.

"Huston-Tillotson University has a rich and remarkable history," stated Dr. Colette Pierce Burnette, the first female President and Chief Executive Officer of the merged Huston-Tillotson University. "It is a gift to be a part of its continuing legacy. It is an honor to serve the genius generation and watch them ascend to excellence during their matriculation on campus. We don't graduate individuals—we graduate families."

While small in size, the reach and impact of the institution are large in scope. HT is home to a variety of initiatives and programs that curate unique learning opportunities and community engagement. Among them are:

- All-Steinway School
- Center for Academic Excellence
- Center for Academic Innovation and Transformation
- AusPrep: Pre-Engineering Program
- Master of Business Administration and Master of Education
- Green is the New Black – Environmental Justice
- W.E.B. Du Bois, St. David's, and Merck Scholars

While offering a variety of future-forward programs, HT is deeply committed to

Changing the World

ON THE MORNING OF SEPTEMBER 15, 1883, THE UNIVERSITY OF TEXAS AT AUSTIN OPENED WITH ONE BUILDING, EIGHT PROFESSORS, ONE PROCTOR, AND 221 STUDENTS. THOUGH SMALL IN STATURE, THE NEW SCHOOL HAD AN AMBITIOUS MISSION—TO CHANGE THE WORLD.

It has done exactly that.

The flagship institution of the University of Texas System, UT Austin today is a world-renowned higher education, research, and public service institution ranked among the 40 best universities in the world. The university serves more than 51,000 students annually through 18 top-ranked colleges and schools.

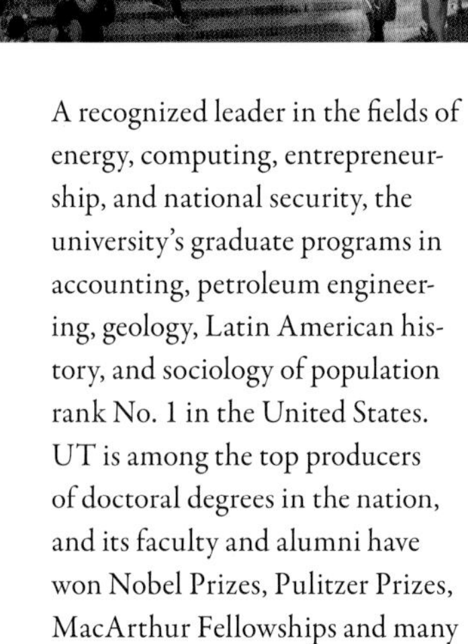

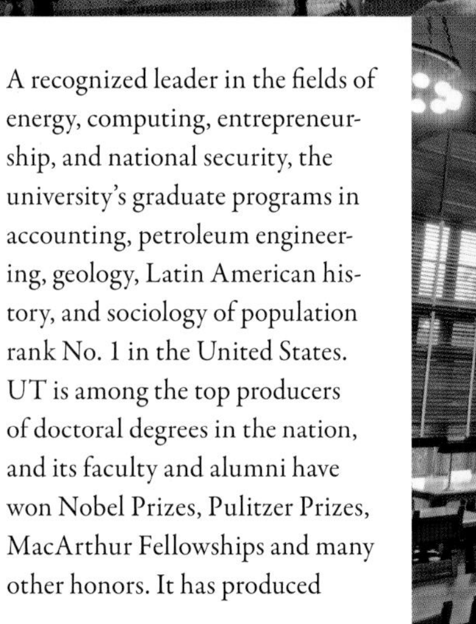

A recognized leader in the fields of energy, computing, entrepreneurship, and national security, the university's graduate programs in accounting, petroleum engineering, geology, Latin American history, and sociology of population rank No. 1 in the United States. UT is among the top producers of doctoral degrees in the nation, and its faculty and alumni have won Nobel Prizes, Pulitzer Prizes, MacArthur Fellowships and many other honors. It has produced dozens of Fulbright, Rhodes, Marshall, and Truman scholars.

GROWING WITH AUSTIN

The university was signed into law by Governor Oran Roberts and was located in Austin by a statewide vote. From the original 40-acre tract set aside by the Legislature, UT's Main Campus now stretches across 431 acres near downtown with more than 150 buildings encompassing upwards of 18 million square feet of space. In addition, there is the even larger J.J. Pickle Research Campus in north Austin, the Lady Bird Johnson Wildflower Center in south Austin, the McDonald Observatory in west Texas, the Marine Science Institute in Port Aransas, and several cultural and historic sites across the state.

By law, 90 percent of each freshman class must be Texas residents, but the student body typically includes residents from all 50 states and more than 140 foreign countries. Aside from state government, UT is the largest employer in Austin with almost 18,000 full and part-time employees, 3,300 of whom are faculty members, and 11,800 part-time student employees.

A FOCUS ON STUDENTS

UT supports students through 15 career centers, more than 400 study-abroad programs, student success initiatives, and more than 1,300 student organizations. Its four-year graduation rate is nearly 70 percent and its six-year graduation rate is more than 85 percent.

The new Texas Advance Commitment completely covers tuition and fees for students from families that earn up to $65,000 a year with financial need, and provides some assured tuition support to students from families with incomes of up to $125,000 who have financial need.

Students are drawn into the inescapable "Longhorn Tradition" from their earliest days on campus. For some, it is the roar of the burnt-orange crowd on an autumn football Saturday in storied 100,000-seat Darrell K Royal-Texas Memorial Stadium. UT student-athletes, now competing in the Big XII Conference, have won more than

50 national championships and 130 Olympic medals.

For others, it's finding that peaceful spot for studying tucked away in a library full of literary treasures, including a Gutenberg Bible and other rare books, manuscripts, photographs, artworks and artifacts from natural history to pop culture in eight museums and 17 libraries.

For many, it is the solemn pride felt in singing "The Eyes of Texas." Written by two UT students and adopted as the university's alma mater in 1903, the song embodies the spirit of the students, faculty, and staff of The University of Texas at Austin.

A Focus on Community

As a member of the Austin community, UT takes great pride in the role it plays in improving the quality of life in the region and creating a vibrant Texas. In 2016, Texas became the first major U.S. university in 50 years to open a new medical school when the Dell Medical School welcomed its first class. It is impossible now to envision Austin without UT Dell Med and its focus on improving public health in Travis County and transforming health globally.

The University of Texas Elementary School is a charter school allowing East Austin students to benefit from UT students and faculty. Additionally, UT works to improve k-12 education, and its UTeach teacher certification program, focusing on secondary mathematics, science, and computer science teachers, is a nationally recognized model.

A member of the prestigious Association of American Universities since 1929, UT attracts more than $650 million annually for research. Through a succession of large grants from the National Science Foundation, UT has built a series of the fastest supercomputers for open research, including Frontera, the most powerful supercomputer at any university in the world. The Department of Defense has designated UT's Applied Research Laboratories as one of five University Affiliated Research Centers, and the university is a major collaborator with the Army Futures Command with partnerships in robotics and assured positioning.

More than 900 freshmen participate each year in the Freshman Research Initiative in UT's College of Natural Science. The program is a shining example of what studying at a top research university can mean for students from the very start of their college careers. The university believes that giving undergraduate students an authentic research experience is key to their development.

"At The University of Texas, we continually strive to reach our own potential, and we do that by unlocking

the potential of all who come here to teach, work, and learn," says President Gregory L. Fenves. "That's how we rise to the heights we are capable of and live up to those six words that define us – what starts here changes the world."

utexas.edu

Customer Driven. Community Focused.

AUSTIN ENERGY BEGAN LIGHTING A BRIGHTER FUTURE FOR THE AUSTIN AREA IN 1895. TODAY, MORE THAN 1,700 DEDICATED EMPLOYEES FOCUS ON FULFILLING THE UTILITY'S COMMITMENT TO SAFELY DELIVER CLEAN, AFFORDABLE, RELIABLE ENERGY AND EXCELLENT CUSTOMER SERVICE—24 HOURS A DAY, 365 days a year—to more than 490,000 customers across a 437-square mile area across Central Texas.

Though its home in the Texas capital, Austin Energy has an effect throughout the state. Austin Energy is invested in carbon-free generation all across Texas, including Far West and East Texas as well as the Texas Coast. The utility invests in the communities served through innovative programs such as energy efficiency programs, rooftop and community solar, and an award-winning Customer Assistance Program. Austin Energy's operations light a better future for Austin and 14 surrounding communities by supporting the sustainability of the state as a whole.

Austin Energy was created by the community. Voters in 1890 passed a bond election to build a hydroelectric dam and powerhouse to create a more controlled water supply and a source for generating electricity. Those voters believed that a utility owned by the community would help keep prices down and bring jobs to Austin.

On May 6, 1895, switches were thrown to illuminate the 31 original moonlight towers. The now iconic structures were a truly historic way to mark the start of the city's electric utility. Today, Austin Energy continues that tradition, being the only city in the world that still maintains and operates its remaining towers. With 17 remaining towers, visitors can still gaze in wonder at the soft, blue "artificial moonlight" that shines over a city rich in historical heritage.

The goal of those visionaries has been realized. Austin Energy has helped build a better Austin by harnessing electric power to provide value, and support affordability, job growth, and customer and community benefits. Austin has prospered by owning and controlling its own electric utility, keeping Austin on the cutting edge of technology. Austin is seen as a destination city in part because Austin Energy has helped spur economic development and delivered reliable energy for more than a century.

AN IMPRESSIVE PORTFOLIO

Austin Energy has a generation portfolio of more than 4,600 megawatts of generation capacity from both traditional and renewable sources. As part of the Electric Reliability Council of Texas' wholesale market, Austin Energy buys all the electricity customers need from the market and sells electricity produced by its plants and contracts into the market. Austin Energy manages and maintains more than 12,000 miles of power lines to make sure customers get the power they need from the state-wide grid. And the utility has dedicated staff and crew members to make sure lights come on—even after a storm.

Austin Energy has provided service to the area for almost 125 years, and its success is tied to those it serves. In an ever-changing environment, the utility strives to safely meet customers' needs and exceed their expectations in providing electricity and beneficial programs. This is the kind of collabo-

▲ Jackie A. Sargent, Austin Energy General Manager

ration that builds a stronger utility and stronger communities.

Surpassing those goals and exceeding expectations did not just happen. Remaining on the cutting edge of technology, efficient operations, and effective market management have been key to Austin Energy's ability to increase its renewable energy portfolio.

To keep up with the downtown growth, Austin Energy is Repowering Downtown. The project supports reliability, outage prevention and increases system capacity to account for the growth of the downtown community. This includes upgrading existing electrical equipment and building new infrastructure with robust community engagement.

Focused on the Future

Austin Energy is proud to be a pioneer for sustainable, clean energy.

In 1995, the utility invested in the first commercial wind farm in Texas and continues to lead the way in utility environmental excellence. Austin Energy is on target to offset 65 percent of customers' energy needs with renewable resources by 2027. Successful operations in generation and market management increase the value that Austin Energy brings to the community.

Austin Energy wants its customers' utility bills to be as low as possible. According to 2017 federal data from the Energy Information Administration, Austin Energy residential customers came in below state averages for comparable electric utilities in both usage and customer bills.

Often, the best way to save money on an electricity bill is to find ways to reduce consumption. Austin Energy helps customers do just that by providing a wide array of rebates and incentives to help customers make energy efficiency improvements to their homes and offices. One example is Austin Energy Green Building. Created in 1990, it was the nation's first ever green building program and is one of the most successful sustainable building programs.

The driving force behind Austin Energy's achievements is its commitment to being Customer Driven and Community Focused. The utility will continue to drive customer value in energy services with innovative technology and environmental leadership.

Design That Makes Lives Better

FOUNDED BY TWO BROTHERS IN A SMALL DOWNTOWN OFFICE IN 1898, PAGE HAS SHAPED BUILDINGS AND URBAN SPACES OF AUSTIN FOR MOST OF THE CITY'S HISTORY. TODAY, IT IS A GLOBAL MULTIDISCIPLINARY ARCHITECTURE, ENGINEERING, AND DESIGN FIRM WITH MORE THAN 650 EMPLOYEES ACROSS THE COUNTRY AND ABROAD.

Still located downtown and still shaping the Austin landscape, the firm has designed buildings on more than 27 blocks in the central business district alone. It promises design that makes lives better and prides itself on its role in the growth and success of its hometown.

▲ Austin Convention Center
Photo by R. Greg Hursley

▶ Austin Bergstrom Iinternational Airport
Photo by John Edward Linden Photography

AN ENDURING LEGACY

The legacy of Page begins with Page Brothers Architects started by Charles Henry Page, Jr. and Louis Page. Significant early landmarks include the Texas Pavilion at the 1904 St. Louis World's Fair and the Littlefield Building, which was briefly the tallest building between New Orleans and San Francisco after its completion in 1912. The firm's early portfolio includes projects ranging from the first public schools in Texas to a number of courthouses across the state as well as commercial office buildings and single-family residences. As the city grew, the firm and its portfolio expanded, under the name Page Southerland Page, to meet the wide variety of development needs.

During the late 20th century, as Austin began to re-envision its future and its growth while still keeping it weird, the firm continued to influence and contribute to the city's success. The firm's completion of the Austin Convention Center and the Barbara Jordan Terminal at Austin Bergstrom International Airport were important symbols of the city. The seeds of what would become a livable, walkable downtown were planted with the Second Street District and its first buildings, including the Page offices in the Silicon Labs buildings and anchoring residential developments.

More recently, the firm shortened its name to just Page and has designed numerous mixed-use office towers and residential high-rises downtown, notably in the Rainey Street District where two Page-designed towers will be done by 2021. Further north at the Texas Capitol Complex and The University of Texas at Austin, Page is also impacting the future of the government and academia. For the Capitol Complex, the firm completed a masterplan for the 40-block district reimagining it with a new six-acre urban park.

"With a 121-year history, we have shaped Austin and it has shaped us," states Robert Burke, Page Senior Principal. "Our work, which includes both iconic and quieter buildings throughout town, has been part of the growth and evolution of the urban core. We're the lucky ones who get to take our clients' ideas—be it The University of Texas, the state and municipal governments, the school district or private developers, corporations, institutions, and community organizations—and create beautiful spaces where they can

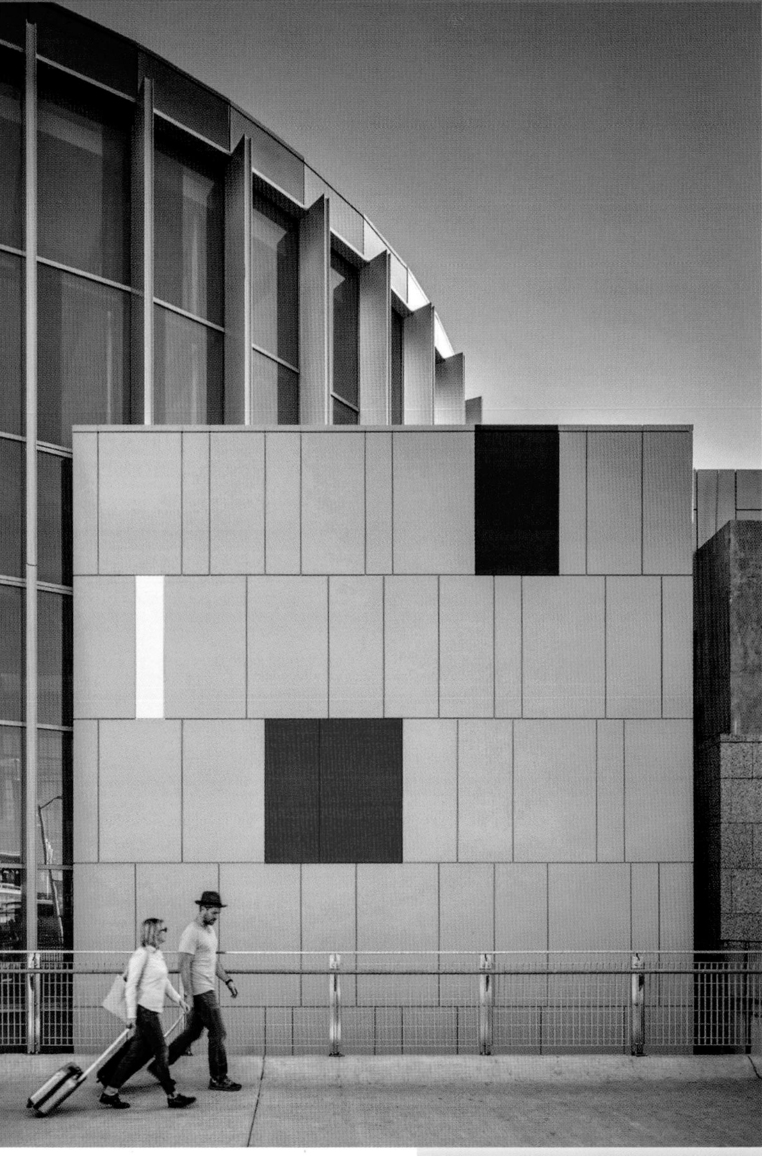

◀ Austin Bergstrom Iinternational Airport
Photo by Tim Griffith Photography

the first medical school to be built from the ground up at a Tier One university in 50 years. Honored with numerous design awards, Dell Medical School supports a team-based learning approach uncommon in medical education, facilitating an integrated and community-based medical practice. It is quickly transforming how medicine is both taught and practiced.

Another transformative local project designed by Page is Magnolia Montessori For All, the first public Montessori school in the Austin Independent School District. The project, which is located in an underserved community in northeast Austin, was recognized with local, regional, and national de-
(continued on next page)

▼ Dell Medical School
Photo by Dror Baldinger FAIA Photography

realize their missions. The airport, for example, is the gateway to the city and thus reflects the values and the culture here. Likewise, the Second Street District has been fundamental to the transformation of Austin as an attractive live-work-play city with an increasing international appeal."

Helping Shape the City's Landscape

The Texas Mall, which will occupy Congress Avenue, between 15th Street and Martin Luther King Jr. Boulevard, will be a native plant-filled green space that serves as a gathering area for state employees and the larger community of Austin. State employees will also benefit from two new buildings designed by Page adding 1,000,000 new square feet of office space to the district.

For Dell Medical School at The University of Texas, Page helped design the masterplan for the 6.5 million-square-foot addition to the campus and four of its buildings, establishing

▲ Austin Convention Center
Photo by Casey Dunn Photography

▶ Dell Medical School
Photo by Dror Baldinger FAIA Photography

sign awards. It was also honored with a community impact award.

A Unique Approach

Page is uniquely positioned among American architectural firms in its ability to combine master planning, urban design, and individual building execution to produce powerful places. For several decades, the firm has sustained involvement over long periods of time in planning and building important urban districts across the country, and especially in Austin. Page integrates planning, urban design, architecture, engineering, interiors, and branding into a seamless, continuous whole.

This interdisciplinary and integrated approach to design means that architects, engineers, interior designers, strategic consultants, urban planners, urban designers, landscape architects, lab planners, graphic designers, and experiential designers are all working together. Page targets seven market sectors: academic, aviation, civic/government, corporate/commercial, healthcare, housing/hospitality, and science and technology. The company has robust teams working on all project types that fall into these sectors. The Austin office has more than 250 employees and is the largest of the nine offices in Dallas, Denver, Dubai, Houston, Mexico City, Phoenix, Washington D.C., and San Francisco.

The firm ranks in the country's top architectural and engineering design firms and has been honored with more than 400 design awards. Locally, it was recognized as AIA Austin's Architecture Firm of the Year in 1997 and was the Texas Society of Architects Firm of the Year in 2009. Nationally, it is consistently ranked in the top architecture firms by Architect and Architectural Record magazines.

"We're grounded in what makes Austin special," Burke adds.

"Our team knows that the work we are doing now to create the new Texas Mall at the Capitol Complex will be a green space for the city to enjoy for generations. We're thinking about improving the future of the city every day."

A Community Partner

The firm is dedicated to the Austin community and volunteers numerous hours to local associations and non-profits. It continues to support the UMLAUF Sculpture Garden and Museum since designing its facility in 1991. Current collaborators include Austin Habitat for Humanity, for which Page is designing the largest mixed-use residential development to be built by the organization in the country.

Page employees are very active on local boards and are leaders in organizations such as AIA Austin, Texas Society of Architects, Urban Land Institute, and Meals On Wheels, among others.

"Ultimately," Burke notes, "it is not only our work on the buildings and urban spaces that have contributed to the success and growth of the Austin area, it is our people. We're on not-for-profit boards. We teach at and support The University of Texas and other local academic institutions. We volunteer for associations and participate in community activities. We coach Little League. Our employees are shaping the city in their everyday and professional lives."

▶ Wiss, Janney, Elstner Associates Office Building
Photo by Casey Dunn Photography

▼ Texas Capitol Complex Master Plan

Compassionate, Personalized Care for All

SINCE FIRST OPENING ITS DOORS IN AUSTIN IN 1902, ASCENSION SETON HAS GROWN FROM AN INFIRMARY TO A NETWORK OF 11 HOSPITALS AND MORE THAN 100 CLINICAL LOCATIONS ACROSS CENTRAL TEXAS. ASCENSION SETON IS PART OF ASCENSION, ONE OF THE NATION'S LEADING NON-PROFIT HEALTH SYSTEMS, SERVING PATIENTS through a network of hospitals, providers, and related health facilities providing acute care services, long-term care, community health services, psychiatric, rehabilitation, and residential care.

While the healthcare services offered by Ascension Seton have expanded dramatically from that first 40-bed hospital opened in 1902, Ascension's mission has remained the same as when the Daughters of Charity of St. Vincent de Paul founded the nucleus of the organization in 17th Century France - expressing God's love through services to the sick, the poor, and the destitute. The original sponsoring organizations of the healthcare ministries which came together as Ascension established a foundation that continues shaping its work today. Ascension is committed to caring for those who are most in need in our communities.

A LEGACY OF SERVICE

Those early visionaries of three centuries ago became the first non-cloistered community of religious women working in the streets and homes doing God's work. The Daughters came to America largely through the efforts of Elizabeth Ann Seton, a widow who established a religious community in Maryland and adopted the philosophy of St. Vincent de Paul.

Today, the Daughters of Charity are an international community of over 18,000 Catholic women ministering all over the world. The Daughters of Charity still serve the "poorest of the poor." Their ministry touches those in need through education, healthcare, social, and pastoral services. Prayer and

community life are essential elements for their vocation of service.

In Texas, Ascension operates Ascension Providence and Ascension Seton, which includes Dell Children's Medical Center, the region's only comprehensive children's hospital and pediatric Level I trauma center, and Dell Seton Medical Center at The University of Texas, the region's only Level I trauma center for adults. Ascension Seton partners with Dell Medical School at The University of Texas at Austin and shares a common vision of transforming healthcare through a focus on quality and value.

Ascension remains a faith-based healthcare organization committed to delivering compassionate, personalized care to all, with special attention to persons living in poverty and those most vulnerable.

Compassionate and Personalized Care

Ascension Seton offers convenient locations throughout the Austin area, offering easy access to primary, emergency, and specialty care when and where it is needed. Specialty services include:

- Highest level of trauma care—Level 1 at Dell Children's and Dell Seton
- Highest level of NICU care
- Online Care – 24/7 access to doctors
- Online scheduling for physician appointments, express care, and emergency care
- Dell Children's Emergency Care available at other Ascension Seton hospital locations – Ascension Seton Northwest, Ascension Seton Williamson, Ascension Seton Hays, and Ascension Seton Southwest
- Only comprehensive pediatric hospital in the region and the greatest number of pediatric specialists
- A partnership with Dell Medical School at The University of Texas at Austin
- Complex brain and spine care
- Only heart transplant program in Central Texas

A Fabric of the Local Community

Ascension believes in relationships and partnerships. Together with over 13,000 associates, Ascension leadership looks forward to continuing our legacy of providing transformational healthcare services in the region.

Part of that vision has been Ascension Seton's support for the creation of the Dell Medical School, the first Tier 1 U.S. research university in nearly half a century. Ascension Seton's unique partnership with the university and the medical school to shape its signature curriculum and research efforts, which include a focus on creating a more efficient and effective healthcare system and training future physician leaders.

Working together, Ascension Seton and the medical school are establishing and expanding key clinical programs right here in Austin so individuals and families can stay close to home for care.

Another critical component of this partnership was the addition of a $260 million, 211-bed teaching hospital in downtown Austin in 2017. Dell Seton Medical Center at The University of Texas is the centerpiece of a new health district in the heart of the city and anchors a new healthcare innovation zone in downtown Austin. This area is expected to attract research facilities, entrepreneurs, and other innovators in the life sciences.

In addition, Dell Seton Medical Center, Ascension Seton Medical Center Austin, Dell Children's Medical Center, and Ascension Shoal Creek make up the network of teaching hospitals for the medical school. To find compassionate, personalized care near you, please visit healthcare.ascension.org

Paul McCarthy, "White Snow #3" (detail), 2012. Artwork © Paul McCarthy. Courtesy of The Contemporary Austin - Laguna Gloria

Photo by Noah Towery

SAM, LLC

Setting the Standard for a Quarter Century

WITH ONLY $250 IN HIS POCKETS, SAMIR "SAM" G. HANNA LEFT HIS HOME IN EGYPT AND CAME TO THE U.S. IN 1970. WHILE HE MAY HAVE HAD LIMITED FUNDS, HE POSSESSED A STRONG WORK ETHIC AND A DREAM OF FINANCIALLY SUPPORTING HIS FAMILY. PURSUIT OF THAT DREAM LED HANNA TO BUILD what has become one of the largest and most successful geospatial and construction phase services companies in North America. Headquartered in Austin, SAM (for Surveying and Mapping), LLC today employs 1,100 highly skilled experts located in 29 offices nationwide. The firm has become an undisputed leader in its field, serving a wide variety of industries.

Chris M. Solomon, RPLS, is currently the President and CEO of the company. Having been with SAM since its founding in 1994, Solomon has deep experience with all aspects of the firm's history and business. In 2014, a group of investors led by Joe Aragona with Austin Ventures, Austin's most experienced venture capital/private equity firm, became investment partners with SAM.

Sam Hanna currently serves as Chairman of the Board of Directors, and the company is celebrating its 25-year anniversary in 2019.

Solomon noted several keys to the company's success: "SAM has grown into the largest company of its kind in the country due to our entrepreneurial spirit, our commitment to advanced technology, and our focus on hiring the very best people in our industry."

From the beginning SAM has maintained a sharp focus on diversification of services, clients, and geographic range. These fundamentals continue to be keys to the company's success. Today SAM offers a full range of geospatial services, including professional land surveying, airborne/mobile/terrestrial LiDAR, Geographic Information Systems (GIS), Subsurface Utility Engineering (SUE), Utility Coordination (UC), Building Information Modeling (BIM), aerial mapping, and photogrammetry. SAM also provides construction phase services through its wholly owned subsidiary, SAM-Construction Services, LLC.

Another integral part of SAM's success has been its commitment to investing in advanced technology. Practically every emerging technology in their industry was adopted by SAM early on and then applied to the greatest effect to meet client needs.

SAM continues to build on its foundational strengths. In addition to continued organic growth, the company has made three strategic acquisitions in the last three years, compounding its expansion across both service and regional areas.

According to Aragona, "When we became an investment partner with the management team at SAM, we saw great potential for a bold, aggressive growth for the company, and we have not been disappointed. SAM's industry leading position and exceptional execution for its clients in its core markets continues to support additional expansion and growth for the future."

PROUD TO CALL AUSTIN HOME

SAM has been recognized repeatedly as one of Austin's "Top Work Places" by the American-Statesman, and ranks among the Austin Business Journal's largest private firms in the greater Austin area.

According to Solomon, "We're proud to be a strong partner in supporting the Austin community. We employ nearly 400 people in Austin, and contribute to the region through both community engagement and our continued business growth. Austin is our home, and we're enthusiastic about doing our part to keep it a vibrant, thriving community."

Aligned by industry. Built on relationships.

One of Austin's longest-standing law firms, Husch Blackwell, services an impressive list of prestigious corporate clients. The firm has been—and continues to be—built around a single idea: to guide the clients from where they are to where they want to be.

The firm's unique industry-centric approach results in a deep understanding of what their clients face every day. More than that, it creates a shared vision that moves each client forward.

Husch Blackwell has a strong national presence with offices in 18 cities and 700 plus attorneys. The Austin office, located just steps away from the Texas State Capitol and courthouses in Austin's Central Business District, has its own unique history and culture. The office features a hard working and fun group of over 60 lawyers, including Texas State Senator Kirk Watson, and 40 full time staff members, some of whom have been with the firm for more than 40 years and all of whom are an integral part of the firm's success. The firm's approach to law—"Aligned by industry. Built on relationships"—reflects not only a commitment to providing top quality legal work and client service, but also to developing our lawyers, staff, and future leaders; fostering a diverse workplace; and taking on a leadership role in the community.

Rooted in over a century of service

Over 100 years ago in Kansas City, Missouri, Henry McCune, Robert Caldwell and Blatchford Downing began laying the foundation for what would eventually become Husch Blackwell. The firm of Brown McCarroll was established in Austin, Houston, and Dallas in 1938. Over the years, through steady growth and expansion, both firms attracted clients and prospered, ultimately joining forces in 2013. Today, Husch Blackwell is ranked by the *National Law Journal* as the 79th largest firm in the United States.

While Husch Blackwell is the product of many predecessor firms hailing from across the country, the firm is unified around a unique industry and a dedication to client service. In 2012, the firm dispensed with traditional legal practice areas and organized itself into industry groups in order to drive greater engagement with its clients' business challenges. The industry teams—Energy & Natural Resources; Financial Services & Capital Markets; Food & Agribusiness; Healthcare, Life Sciences & Education; Real Estate, Development & Construction; and Technology, Manufacturing & Transportation—allow the firm to field interdisciplinary teams that bring

together exactly the skills and resources each client needs.

Husch Blackwell is widely recognized by clients on a national level for its consistently high quality of service and value. By implementing an industry¬based approach, the firm's lawyers have developed a deep understanding of each client's business and respond with real world solutions designed to achieve business objectives in the most efficient manner possible on both a local and national level. In addition to Austin, the firm's network of offices comprises 17 cities, including:

- Chattanooga, Tennessee
- Chicago, Illinois
- Dallas, Texas
- Denver, Colorado
- Houston, Texas
- Jefferson City, Missouri
- Kansas City, Missouri
- Lincoln, Nebraska
- Madison, Wisconsin
- Milwaukee, Wisconsin
- Omaha, Nebraska
- Phoenix, Arizona
- Sacramento, California
- Springfield, Missouri
- St. Louis, Missouri
- Washington, D.C.
- Waukesha, Wisconsin

Legal industry innovators

In addition to its bold, industry based reconfiguration, Husch Blackwell is a recognized leader in the legal industry in developing innovative products, services, and approaches to the practice of law. The firm's wholly¬owned subsidiary, HB Innovations, is charged with organizing and developing a wide ranging program that uses cutting edge technologies, such as artificial intelligence and advanced legal project management techniques (LPM), to improve outcomes and reduce costs.

The firm's value driven focus ensures seamless partnering with clients to develop practical solutions. The Legal Project Management Team delivers value and transparency by carefully scoping, planning, monitoring, and reviewing legal matters; ensuring efficiency and a streamlined workload; and the proactive identification and removal of obstacles. Among law firms serving *Fortune* 1000 and other large clients, Husch Blackwell has received industry wide recognition for developing and implementing innovative alternative fee arrangements. The firm offers a variety of options that foster trust and transparency around legal fees, including fixed or flat fees, risk¬sharing arrangements, alternative hourly rates, and hybrid fee arrangements.

In 2018, Husch Blackwell received (for the second consecutive year) the Association of Corporate Counsel's Value Champion award, an accolade which recognizes collaborations that deliver substantial value to their clients' organizations by cutting spending, improving predictability, and achieving better legal results. This dedication to delivering excellent outcomes earns the trust and respect of clients far and wide.

(continued next page)

Husch Blackwell LLP

Carey Bartell, Vice President and Chief Legal Counsel with Conagra Brands, one of the largest packaged foods companies in the world, recently remarked, "The Husch Blackwell team's expertise in the substantive legal issues, combined with the investment they made to develop a deep knowledge of our business, has made them a uniquely effective litigation partner."

Justice for All

While the lawyers of Husch Blackwell have a well established reputation for their business acumen and sound judgment, they also have maintained a strong focus on giving back to the communities in which they live and work. Providing pro bono legal services to the needy is a cornerstone of the firm's culture and is widely considered an essential part of maintaining a private law practice. The firm provides tens of thousands of hours of free legal services each year, supporting a variety of worthy causes, including childhood health and education, veterans' rights and benefits, civil rights, criminal justice reform, and economic development in disadvantaged neighborhoods. Husch Blackwell remains committed to sharing the skills of its team members to advance access to justice and to help hundreds of non profit organizations achieve their goals.

Leadership Through Diversity

Husch Blackwell's sponsorship initiative increases diversity at the firm's highest ranks by promoting talented attorneys from under represented groups. The initiative matches select senior associates and new partners with senior level sponsors. Sponsors foster success by touting protégés to colleagues and clients, securing high visibility work assignments, including them in business development, directing business to them, and helping them make progress toward quantitative standards for advancement.

The firm's Women's Initiative recognizes the vital role that law firms play in creating and maintaining the conditions in which women can thrive in the practice of law. Husch Blackwell proudly offers professional development opportunities and events designed to increase leadership roles for female attorneys and law students. The Initiative's True North program brings women together from across the firm—as well as clients—through networking events and professional development opportunities.

Being inclusive is an integral part of how we do business, both internally and externally. In concert with Husch Blackwell's written diversity policy, more than 50 diversity council and committee members set goals, which are executed by the highest levels of firm leadership, including the firm's chairman, CEO, and executive board, impacting a wide variety of operations, including professional development, recruiting, and procurement.

Our diversity and inclusion efforts have garnered recognition, including:

- Mansfield Certification Plus designation for 2019 from Diversity Lab
- Austin Law Firm Diversity Report Card, Grade A
- Houston Bar Association's Gender Fairness Commitment, Signatory
- Women Inc. magazine's "Top 100 Firms for Women" for 2019
- 2019 Corporate Equality Index, Perfect Score, Human Rights Campaign Foundation

Part of the Fabric of Austin For More Than 95 Years

As Austin grew from what was a small town in Central Texas to become the state's political and cultural capital and an epicenter for both the arts and technology, so, too, has St. David's HealthCare evolved into one of the top healthcare systems in the U.S. Chartered by the State of Texas in 1924 and named after St. David's Episcopal Church, the healthcare system's reach is felt across the globe. In addition to treating patients in the Central Texas Region, people seeking specialized care at St. David's HealthCare facilities and institutes travel here from around the world.

▲ St. David's Medical Center today.

St. David's HealthCare operates 132 sites across Central Texas, including eight hospitals:

- St. David's Medical Center
- St. David's North Austin Medical Center
- St. David's South Austin Medical Center
- St. David's Round Rock Medical Center
- St. David's Georgetown Hospital
- Heart Hospital of Austin
- St. David's Rehabilitation Hospital
- St. David's Surgical Hospital

A Unique Partnership

St. David's HealthCare operates as a joint venture partnership between HCA Healthcare, one of the nation's leading providers of healthcare services, and two local non-profits—St. David's Foundation and Georgetown Health Foundation. St. David's Foundation is a philanthropic organization aimed at investing in the community to create healthier lives for all Central Texans by addressing the region's top health challenges. The proceeds from hospital operations fund the foundations, which, in turn, invest those dollars back into the community. Since the inception of St. David's HealthCare in 1996, more than $518 million have been given back to the community to improve the health and healthcare of Central Texans.

Commitment to Excellence

"St. David's HealthCare is committed to being the finest care and service organization in the world, and we continue to raise the bar and push ourselves to be the very best—for our patients, physicians, employees, and our community," stated David Huffstutler, President and CEO of St. David's HealthCare.

St. David's staff of more than 10,600 people (the third largest private employer in the Austin area), who are supported by an additional 2,300 medical staff members, live that commitment daily. And their achievement of their goal to be the best in their field has been noted. The organization was honored with a Malcolm Baldrige National Quality Award, the nation's highest presidential honor for performance excellence and the first healthcare system in Texas to earn it. Additionally, St. David's HealthCare facilities have individually earned national recognition for providing exceptional patient care. For example, St. David's Medical Center - in conjunction with its Heart Hospital of Austin and St. David's Georgetown Hospital campuses - has been named among the nation's 100 Top Hospitals by IBM Watson Health™ for ten consecutive years.

With the most advanced clinical protocols, surgical technologies, and dedicated professional staff, St. David's HealthCare continues its focus on ensuring the best clinical outcomes for its patients.

▼ St. David's Hospital in 1924

Faith, Learning, & Life-Changing Experiences

Founded in 1926, Concordia University Texas is Austin's leading Christian university. The independent, liberal arts school is ingrained into a century of Austin's history and is an essential part of the city's future. Beginning as a high school to prepare young men for ministry, Concordia's original campus was built on East Avenue in downtown Austin, long before the concrete

decks of I-35 existed. The University first admitted women in 1955, and, in 2008, Concordia moved to the former Schlumberger campus in Northwest Austin.

Concordia strives to be a place where Christ is honored and all are welcome. Christian faith drives what Concordia does, and from it flows the University's commitment to serving the Austin community. Through its affiliation with the Lutheran Church-Missouri Synod, the school is part of the Concordia University System, which enrolls over 35,000 students nationwide.

Connecting With the Community

A leader in urban environmentalism, the University owns and manages a 250-acre nature preserve that is part of the Balcones Canyonlands Preserve, with the assistance of Travis County Parks and Wildlife. Additionally, the preserve serves as a research field for students.

The University's size allows students to participate in multiple programs, including music, drama, student government, clubs and other student organizations. The Concordia Community Music Academy offers individualized musical training to the entire community.

Through IncubatorCTX, Concordia connects local entrepreneurs with the resources they need to launch their next great idea, including a place to work and access to experienced mentors. IncubatorCTX events bring community and business leaders together with students, offering rich networking opportunities.

Nursing students learn high-tech skills in the University's simulation labs and further develop their skills by serving at local healthcare facilities in Central Texas. Additionally, the students provide free basic health assessments and education to vulnerable populations in Austin through Concordia's Medical Missions Van.

Between the University's 15 NCAA Division III teams, Concordia has won a total of ten American Southwest Conference (ASC) championships. The excellent athletics program includes world-class baseball and softball fields and is alma mater to successful athletes, including former MLB pitcher Scott Linebrink. The newest addition to varsity athletics, Concordia Esports is the first program of its kind in the Central Texas area.

Greatest Community Impact

Concordia's greatest impact on Austin is made through its graduates, who are recognized in the community as leaders of nonprofits, public and private educators and administrators, successful business owners and more.

The University's liberal arts education prepares graduates to solve complex problems and generate creative solutions. Because of the emphasis on Christian service and meaningful work, Concordia alumni seek ways to use their knowledge and gifts to serve others in Austin, across Texas and all over the world.

For more information about Concordia University Texas, visit www.concordia.edu.

Lower Colorado River Authority

Enhancing the Quality of Life for More Than a Million Texans

THE LOWER COLORADO RIVER AUTHORITY PROVIDES VITAL SERVICES TO TEXANS, INCLUDING GENERATING AND DELIVERING ELECTRICITY, MANAGING WATER SUPPLY IN THE LOWER COLORADO RIVER BASIN, OFFERING OUTDOOR ADVENTURE THROUGH ITS SYSTEM OF PARKS, AND SUPPORTING COMMUNITY DEVELOPMENT.

▲ LCRA has been providing electricity to the Hill Country since the 1930s, and provided the first electric power to most small towns and rural communities in Central Texas. Pictured are transmission line workers in 1950.

The Colorado River is the largest river entirely within Texas, stretching 862 miles from near the Texas Panhandle to near the Gulf of Mexico. The river's watershed – the area of land from which water drains into the river – spans more than 42,000 square miles, about 16 % of the total area of Texas. LCRA manages the lower two-thirds of the river – the roughly 600-mile portion from about 80 miles northwest of San Saba to Matagorda Bay.

◀ Timothy Timmerman serves as the chair of LCRA's Board of Directors. Then-Gov. Rick Perry appointed Timmerman to the Board in February 2008 and named him LCRA Board chair in January 2011. Then-Gov. Perry reappointed him in 2013, and Gov. Greg Abbott reappointed Timmerman in 2019 for a term that expires Feb. 1, 2025.

Offering Solutions

Up to the 1930s, the river was a constant threat. In times of drought it could all but dry up, but when rains fell, it unleashed dangerous floods that inundated our capital city and other downstream communities. Flooding even rose above the iconic Congress Avenue bridge in downtown Austin.

At the same time, rural Central Texans faced an additional problem: the lack of reliable, economical electric service. Investor-owned utilities had focused on serving larger Texas cities, leaving smaller communities in the dark. Some Hill Country communities like Johnson City relied on a small generator that ran for a few hours every evening, and many farms and ranches had no electric service at all. In fact, many rural residents of the early 20th century lived and worked much like their ancestors of 100 years earlier.

▼ LCRA operates six dams along the Colorado River. Mansfield Dam, pictured here, creates Lake Travis.

On November 13, 1934, Texas Governor Miriam "Ma" Ferguson signed legislation creating the Lower Colorado River Authority and granting it authority to store and sell water, generate electricity, help reduce flood damages, and implement reforestation and soil-conservation programs. LCRA opened its doors for business on February 19, 1935, and, over the next two decades, built the six dams that created the six Highland Lakes along the Colorado River northwest of Austin.

▼ LCRA Transmission Services Corporation is a nonprofit corporation for transmission operations established in 2002. Since its creation, LCRA TSC has invested billions of dollars in transmission projects to meet the growing demand for electricity, improve reliability, connect new generating capacity, address congestion problems that affect the competitive market and help move renewable energy to the market.

Continuously Serving Texans

Through the years, LCRA's mission has expanded beyond creating hydroelectric power and managing the river and dams. Today, LCRA is a major wholesale public power provider with a diverse power generation portfolio. LCRA provides its wholesale electric customers with competitively priced power in a market affected by increasingly volatile fuel costs. LCRA Transmission Services Corporation builds and operates electric transmission lines within the state.

▲ LCRA offers outdoor adventures at more than 40 parks along the Colorado River from the Texas Hill Country to the Gulf Coast. The parks provide access to the river, as well as hiking, biking and equestrian trails, kayaking, birding, fishing, boating, zip lining, and much more. Shown here is summer camp fun at McKinney Roughs Nature Park near Bastrop.

LCRA also contributes to Texans' quality of life by providing roughly 11,000 acres of parkland along the lower Colorado River, offering first-class recreational opportunities including fishing, hiking, birding, boating, camping, horseback riding and mountain biking, canoeing and kayaking, swimming, zip lining, and much more. LCRA also has a community grant program that provides grants of up to $50,000 to volunteer fire departments, emergency medical services, school districts, libraries, civic groups, local governments and other nonprofit organizations. The Community Development Partnership Program has awarded more than 1,700 grants totaling more than $45 million. LCRA also contributes to communities through LCRA Steps Forward – an annual day of service during which employees spend time working on projects in communities LCRA serves.

As it has for decades, LCRA also continues to manage the lower Colorado River, which provides water for more than a million people, businesses and industries, power plants and agriculture. The people of LCRA – including its employees, senior management team and Board of Directors, led by Chair Timothy Timmerman – are honored to continue enhancing the quality of life of the Texans we serve through water stewardship, energy and community service.

Building Better Futures

FOUNDED IN 1973 WITH ONE CAMPUS SERVING 1,726 STUDENTS, AUSTIN COMMUNITY COLLEGE (ACC) HAS GROWN TO BECOME A RECOGNIZED LEADER IN HIGHER EDUCATION IN THE U.S. AND INTERNATIONALLY. WHAT BEGAN AS AN EXTRAORDINARY VISION AMONG COMMUNITY LEADERS AND EDUCATION pioneers is today the primary gateway to higher education and career training in the region. Over its 45-year existence, ACC has grown to become one of the largest colleges and universities in the nation. Today, approximately 76,000 students choose ACC annually.

ACC's leadership position has been recognized on numerous fronts across the country. In addition to multiple awards for its advanced facilities and campuses, ACC was recognized in 2013 as an "Achieving the Dream Leader College." The following year, ACC was awarded an "Architect of Change" by E3 Alliance. Accolades continued in 2015 with the Sustainability Award from the Association for the Advancement of Sustainability in Higher Education; a Citation of Excellence from Learning by Design; an Impact Award for Innovation from Urban Land Institute of Austin; an Innovator Award by Campus Technology; and an Exemplar College Award from the Texas Association of Community Colleges/ Texas Success Center.

International recognition began in 2017 when ACC was selected as a member of The League for Innovation in the Community Colleges. The college was designated a Hispanic-Serving Institution in 2013, a federal designation indicating a 25 percent or greater full-time equivalent Hispanic enrollment and was awarded with the Seal of Excelencia in 2019 for its progress toward closing equity gaps and significantly increasing Latino student completion.

SERVING A DYNAMIC REGION

ACC founding President/CEO, Dr. Thomas M. Hatfield, was committed to providing an open-admission policy with flexible entrance requirements and job training as well as university-transfer courses when he led the initiative to establish a multi-campus, open admission college embedded in every corner of the community. Austin had become known as a college town with the University of Texas at Austin. As more individuals from diverse sections of Austin wanted to be involved in its growing economy and politics, there was a need for affordable higher education. Today, with Austin being a hub for innovation and the home to an entire tech ecosystem, the workforce needs of the community demand high-quality and affordable higher education.

Those needs are being met by ACC. Students avail themselves to a wide range of learning opportunities through more than 100 programs in ten areas of study at the college's 11 campuses across its 7,000-square mile service area, which is geographically larger than the state of Connecticut. ACC offers affordable access, through traditional and distance learning modes, to higher education and workforce training, including appropriate applied baccalaureate degrees. It remains the number one college choice among Central Texans and ranks top in Texas for transfer success.

Accredited by the Southern Association of Colleges and Schools in 1978, ACC continues to lead the nation in transforming how students learn. The college provides flexible, accelerated learning opportunities and real-world learning experiences to help students complete their education on-time and graduate workforce-ready. Under

the leadership of President/CEO Dr. Richard M. Rhodes (2011-present), the college implemented guided pathways in 2016 to ensure students receive clear guidance to reach their goals in the most efficient and effective way.

Embracing Cutting-Edge Innovation and Technology

Austin Community College embraces innovation and collaboration to transform lives across the local community. The college strives to expand learning and training opportunities and provide real-world experiences that benefit its students and the region.

Pursuant to that goal, ACC in 2014 pioneered the ACCelerator, the nation's largest high-tech digital learning lab featuring more than 600 individual computer stations. The ACCelerator offers a variety of classes from motion graphics, business, and communications to developmental math, English as a second language, geography, and more. The ACCelerator's success in improving student persistence, retention, and completion has generated national attention and prompted expansions districtwide with ACCelerators now available at four of the college's campuses.

ACC also is home to several incubators designed to fuel industry growth in Austin and bridge gaps in workforce education. The ACC Bioscience Incubator opened in early 2017 and provides valuable wet-lab space and an innovative work environment for life-science entrepreneurs. It's also the first bioscience incubator at a community college. ACC's Fashion Incubator opened in spring 2019 to prepare aspiring designers and established entrepreneurs for success. The 7,500-square-foot facility offers career-technical training, transferable credits, a residency program, leasable space, and more. A manufacturing incubator is expected to open in summer 2020.

In 2018, the ACC Hays Campus opened the Public Safety Training Center (PSTC), which provides advanced training facilities for students in the college's Criminal Justice and other first responders programs.

Community Involvement

In addition to transforming the learning landscape and implementing a college-wide focus on issues of equality and inclusion, ACC is involved in many initiatives that benefit the local community. Students participate in numerous areas of service, including:

- Office of Student Life supports a variety of organizations and community-building events.
- Center for Non-profit Studies offers non-profit workforce and career development in Central Texas.
- Center for Public Policy and Political Studies which provides a unique community college government internship program.
- Support of Amplify Austin and other scholarship fundraising efforts helps the ACC Foundation raise funds to support student scholarships, emergency funds, and program support to the college.

According to the latest economic impact study report, issued in 2019, annual income created by ACC topped more than $1.6 billion on the local economy. Higher wages from skills acquired while attending ACC and increased business output stimulate increases in income across the state, thereby raising prosperity in Texas and expanding the economic base for society as a whole. The average associate degree graduate from ACC will see an increase in earning of $10,800 each year compared to a person with a high school diploma or equivalent working in Texas.

Austin Community College is proud to be living its motto: "Start here. Get there."

Technology Enabling A Better World

ADVANCED MICRO DEVICES (AMD) TRACES ITS HISTORY IN AUSTIN TO 1979, BUT THE COMPANY'S ROOTS GO BACK A DECADE EARLIER TO SILICON VALLEY. IT WAS THERE IN 1969 WHEN AMD WAS FOUNDED AS A START-UP WITH EMPLOYEES FOCUSING ON A SINGLE MISSION — DEVELOPING LEADING-EDGE semiconductor solutions. Those days were the dawn of the semiconductor industry, and for AMD, the beginning of a long-history of high-performance computing and graphics innovation that continues to transform our lives today.

From those modest beginnings, AMD has grown into a global company of more than 10,000 people, achieving many important industry firsts along the way. AMD today develops high-performance computing and visualization products to solve some of the world's toughest and most interesting challenges. It is the only company in the world with both high-performance graphics and high-performance computer technology. Whether in the realm of gaming, VR, AR, artificial intelligence, or cloud computing, today's most in-demand applications require high performance. AMD is proud to have the unique capability to develop solutions that fit this broad spectrum of customer needs.

A COMPANY ON THE CUTTING-EDGE

AMD takes great pride in creating high-performance computing and graphics technologies – the foundational building blocks for PCs, gaming, and the data-center. The semiconductor solutions that AMD creates are designed to help solve some of the world's toughest problems by enabling creators, researchers, inventors, and explorers.

AMD engineers develop leading-edge computing and graphics processors and software solutions that power a variety of applications. From desktop and laptop computers for everyday users and businesses, to video game consoles, medical imaging devices, airplane cockpit displays, digital billboards, data-center servers and supercomputers, AMD technology is everywhere. AMD has brought to market many industry firsts, including the first 1GHz CPU, the first 64-bit x86 processors that are now the standard for PCs

▼ AMD CEO Dr. Lisa Su shows the latest AMD EPYC™ microprocessor for servers

and servers, the first x86 multi-core processor and the first single graphics processing unit (GPU) to deliver one teraflop of compute performance. In 2019, AMD delivered the world's first high-performance GPUs and x86 CPUs built on the most advanced 7nm manufacturing technology.

AMD also has an in-house research team that provides technology direction critical to the company's product portfolio. They also support future-focused projects, including helping develop the Frontier supercomputer for the U.S. Department of Energy. These teams pride themselves on fostering a culture of innovative research that supports and encourages research in the academic community. They also maintain alignment with AMD strategic objectives and close ties to the company's product development teams.

Their diverse research focus areas include:

- High-performance computing
- Energy-efficient computing
- Architectures for big data
- Machine learning

AMD innovations are inspired by life—by people and what they can accomplish with the right technology. The company today remains focused on the vision of its founders—imagining a better world and taking inspiration from its customers to deliver innovative solutions to the challenges and possibilities of the digital age. AMD doesn't create technology for technology's sake. The company innovates for its customers and what they can achieve.

A Success Story in Austin

The Austin area is often nicknamed "Silicon Hills" because of the concentration of semiconductor design companies, including AMD, in the area. AMD embraces the opportunities and responsibilities that come with this recognition. AMD chose Austin as the location for a new manufacturing plant in 1979, its first outside of California. In 2008, AMD expanded its Austin operations to a large corporate presence. That same year, the company announced plans to spin off its manufacturing capabilities to become a design-only firm, and it no longer operates manufacturing plants.

Today, AMD's Austin site is the company's largest operations and R&D site in the U.S. The site's approximate 2,100 employees are focused on

▼ AMD leaders ring the NASDAQ bell on the company's 50th anniversary, May 1, 2019

▲ High-performance AMD EPYC™, AMD Ryzen™ and AMD Radeon™ processors are bringing fresh innovation to the data center, PC and gaming markets

developing innovative technology and supporting the company's corporate functions, like sales, marketing, supply chain, and human resources.

Improving Our World

Hundreds of millions of consumers, leading Fortune 500 businesses, and cutting-edge scientific research facilities around the world rely on AMD technology daily to improve how they live, work, and play. AMD employees in Austin and around the world are focused on building great products that push the boundaries of what is possible.

They have succeeded on numerous fronts. Finding cures for the most common and life-threatening diseases, for example, takes a huge amount of time and effort. Theories need to be devised, potential drug regimens designed, and then there will be years of testing before a new drug can be proven to be effective, safe, and ready to be delivered to patients. It's a complex, time-consuming process of trial and error that would take years if performed using laboratory-based tests alone. But what if that process could be accelerated using simulations on supercomputers to find the drug formulations with the best potential for success before time-consuming clinical trials begin?

Employing AMD EPYC™ processors and Radeon™ Instinct accelerators, Symmetric Computing adapted this approach in its work with medical researchers. That approach resulted in a much faster process of finding potential drugs for the treatment of Alzheimer's, Parkinson's, diabetes, and other diseases.

"You're not going to physically test 100 million chemicals," stated Richard Anderson, President and CTO of Symmetric Computing, Inc. "It's not going to happen. Thanks to AMD's technology... with our platform, we can do the main work via the simulation."

A major beneficiary has been the Venture Development Center at the University of Massachusetts in Boston where one of the company's biggest focuses has been Alzheimer's disease.

This, along with numerous "firsts" and other ground-breaking innovations, has led to peer recognition and awards for AMD, including being named to Thomson Reuters list of "100 Global Tech Leaders" in 2018. The company's track record for workplace performance has also been impressive.

▼ AMD Chief Financial Officer Devinder Kumar

AMD was named to Fast Company's "Best Places to Work For Innovators" and the Bloomberg "Gender Equality Index" in 2019. AMD also made the Human Rights Campaign Corporate Equality Index for three consecutive years beginning in 2017 and Forbes' list of "America's Most Just Companies" in 2017 and 2018.

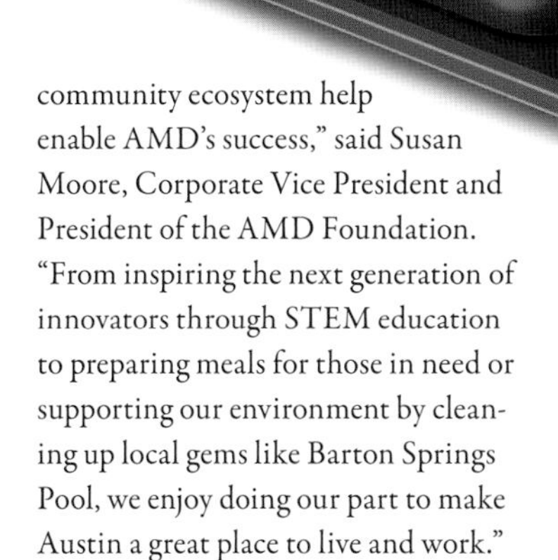

◀ AMD employees volunteer at a park cleanup during the annual AMD Cares Day of Service

▼ AMD employees show local students how a circuit board works during a career-focused event at the AMD campus

On the Home Front

AMD has a deep commitment to the communities in which its employees live and work, and Austin serves as a vital location in AMD's worldwide operations. The company supports the state's thriving technology industry ecosystem through jobs, university relationships, and partnerships with Central Texas charitable organizations.

AMD is recognized as an engaged partner with multiple Austin community organizations that support STEM education, environmental initiatives, and basic community needs. AMD employees—from interns to the C-suite - participate in volunteer activities throughout the year. Since 1995, AMD's workforce worldwide has performed more than 210,000 hours of volunteer service. And, each year, AMD awards charitable grants to local organizations.

"Austin is home to more than 2,000 AMD employees who are passionate about developing and bringing to market high-performance technology, and Austin's creative culture and community ecosystem help enable AMD's success," said Susan Moore, Corporate Vice President and President of the AMD Foundation. "From inspiring the next generation of innovators through STEM education to preparing meals for those in need or supporting our environment by cleaning up local gems like Barton Springs Pool, we enjoy doing our part to make Austin a great place to live and work."

Providing Access to Quality, Affordable Health Care

THERE ARE NUMEROUS REASONS BEHIND THE PHENOMENAL GROWTH OF AUSTIN REGIONAL CLINIC (ARC): THE CONVENIENCE OF SAME-DAY APPOINTMENTS; 24/7 ONLINE APPOINTMENT SCHEDULING; AFTER-HOURS CLINICS OPERATING 365 DAYS A YEAR; POPULATION HEALTH PROGRAMS; Connected Senior Care Advantage (Medicare Advantage program); ARC Healthiness; eMD Access (telemedicine); and acceptance of over 50 health plans.

▲ Dr. Anas Daghestani, CEO, Executive Board President, and Population Health & Clinical Quality Medical Director

▼ Dr. Chenven featured on the cover of Modern Physician in 1997

Add ARC's 27 conveniently located clinics in 11 cities spread across three counties in a 3,000-square-mile area in Central Texas, and it is easy to see how ARC has grown to become the largest primary care delivery system in Central Texas and one of the top three largest multi-specialty physician practices in the region.

With over 500,000 unique patients and over one million patient visits a year, ARC serves 20 percent of the Austin metro area population and continues to rank in the highest level of customer service as measured by its continuous patient survey.

ARC has been on the Top Workplaces List of the Austin American Statesman for four consecutive years, beginning in 2014, and on the Austin Business Journal's Best Places to Work list for nine years before that. ARC also received the Austin Chamber of Commerce "Customer Service Award" among large businesses in 2011.

▼ Dr. Norman Chenven receiving the Texas Academy of Family Physicians (TAFP) 2016 Physician Emeritus Award, November 13, 2016

A COMMITMENT TO SERVICE

Austin Regional Clinic was founded in 1980 as the vision of Norman H. Chenven, MD. The New York native received his medical degree and entered the healthcare field serving the underserved among us, practicing as a family physician on the Navajo/Hopi Indian reservation in Tuba City, Arizona. Working with a small team of 14 doctors in a multi-specialty setting as part of the U.S. Indian Health service, he helped care for 40,000 people, and decided then that he wanted to work in a group practice.

He and his wife moved to Austin in 1973, where he saw the potential for developing a multi-specialty medical group and providing expanded and integrated healthcare services to the Austin metro area. The capital of the Lone Star State had less than 400,000 residents in those days, but it was fast becoming known as a rapidly growing and vibrant community. Dr. Chenven invited pediatricians Dr. Thomas Zavaleta and Dr. Carol Faget to join him in establishing a group practice focused on providing access to quality, affordable health care. From three physicians in one city in 1980, ARC has grown to 350 physicians in 11 cities in Central Texas, offering primary care (Family Medicine, Internal Medicine, Pediatrics) and 16 other specialties, and is continuing to expand.

RESPONDING TO A GROWING COMMUNITY

Having opened its doors in a time of industry transformation, ARC quickly grew and gained the loyalty of Austin residents. New physicians joined the group and additional facilities opened throughout the area. ARC distinguished itself from most other practices by offering services and conveniences that smaller practices could not afford to offer, and by establishing a system of quality assurance that ensured a high standard of care throughout the organization.

ARC was one of the first group practices in the city to open after-hours clinics and offer triage nursing services throughout the night and on weekends and holidays. ARC also provided urgent care services to their patients before the city exploded with urgent care clinics on every corner. And ARC introduced the "ARC MyChart Patient Portal" in 2013, which features an embedded electronic medical record system that allows patients to actively participate in their own care.

▼ Dr. Norman H. Chenven, Founder, FM physician, and CEO from 1980-2016

◀ ARC opens its 25th clinic in Pflugerville, ARC Kelly Lane, February 2019

Dr. Chenven stepped down as CEO of Austin Regional Clinic in 2016, but retains his title of Founding CEO. He also serves as President and CEO of Covenant Management Systems, ARC's management company, and remains very involved in the day-to-day activities of ARC. Dr. Chenven also continues to serve on various local, state, and national boards and is in demand as a speaker nationally on a wide range of healthcare topics.

Dr. Anas Daghestani, ARC's current CEO, has been with the organization since 2005. Soon after joining ARC, he became Chief of Internal Medicine and helped grow ARC's medical home program as Medical Director of Population Health and Clinical Quality, a position he continues to hold in addition to CEO and President of ARC. Dr. Daghestani has a national reputation for both medical group management and value-based medical care.

ARC continues to respond to patient demand for quality medical care closer to home by opening clinics in fast-growing smaller cities throughout the region. Now nearing 40 years in the community, physician-owned and locally managed ARC remains committed to serving Central Texas.

That commitment extends to a robust donations program whereby ARC contributes to nearly 30 non-profits in the region with an emphasis on funds remaining local. Employees can participate in a matching donations program for causes for which they are passionate and in which they are actively involved. ARC also encourages volunteerism through teams with such programs as Meals on Wheels, and participates in numerous community activities in the 11 cities served by the organization.

"Austin Regional Clinic has taken care of the health of Central Texans for almost 40 years," stated Dr. Daghestani, "with an emphasis on prevention that, in the end, helps save healthcare dollars. We employ nearly 2,000 people who contribute to the communities in which they live and work, and we look forward to expanding our locations and services to continue to meet the needs and demands of this vibrant region."

◀▼ ARC has grown with the community, offering 19 specialties in 11 cities in Central Texas.

▼ Many of today's ARC patients have been seeing ARC doctors since birth.

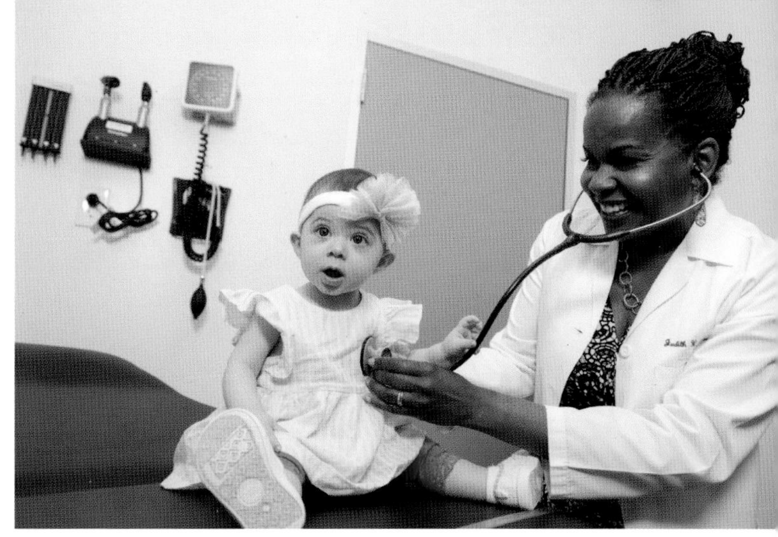

Creating Technologies that Drive Human Progress

IT WAS IN HIS DORM ROOM AT THE UNIVERSITY OF TEXAS IN 1984 THAT MICHAEL DELL RESOLVED TO FOUND A COMPANY THAT WOULD PROVIDE PEOPLE AROUND THE WORLD GREATER ACCESS TO TECHNOLOGY BY RETHINKING HOW COMPUTERS WERE MANUFACTURED AND DELIVERED.

What began in Michael Dell's dorm room more than three decades ago has evolved into an over $90 billion company that is now using technology to drive human progress. Dell Technologies, Inc. has been methodically transforming from a computer hardware manufacturer to an infrastructure solutions provider with significant positions in software and IT services. Dell acquired and successfully integrated multiple companies to expand the company's portfolio, solutions, and services.

In 2013, Michael Dell took the company private in order to invest and make the changes required to shape it into the IT powerhouse it is today. Three years later, Dell then completed a $67 billion acquisition of EMC. On December 28, 2018 Dell returned to the public market under the ticker symbol NYSE:DELL.

AN INDUSTRY LEADER

Dell Technologies employs about 157,000 people across the globe. Approximately 14,000 of those employees are in Central Texas, including at the company's headquarters in Round Rock, a suburb of Austin.

The company today has the industry's broadest and most innovative technology and services portfolio spanning from the edge to the core to the cloud. Dell is known globally as an end-to-end solutions provider with a complimentary portfolio of solutions that demonstrate innovation and drive market performance. As the essential IT infrastructure company for customers, Dell Technologies offers a wide variety of world-class products, solutions, and services to meet its customers digital transformation needs.

Its broad portfolio of solutions helps solve complex problems for customers in the industry's fast-growing areas of hybrid cloud, software-defined data center, converged infrastructure, platform-as-a-service, data analytics, mobility, and cybersecurity. Dell Technologies is positioned better than any other company to help customers adapt to operate in the new digital world.

In addition, Dell's products, solutions and services garnered a record-high 144 product awards and honors at the 2019 Consumer Electronics Show, more than any other company in the industry.

IMPACTING AUSTIN

Dell Technologies has played a key role in helping fuel the growth of Austin and to the city becoming known as a high-tech center dubbed "Silicon Hills." *Forbes* ranked the Austin metropolitan area among the leaders among all big cities for jobs and for growing businesses. Dell continues to have a dramatic impact on the region as indicated by an economic impact study conducted by Dell Technologies in 2017.

According to that study:

- Dell Technologies spends $3.1 billion with local Texas suppliers, and its employees spend much of their $1.7 billion in wages within their local communities.
- Dell Technologies employee wages are 88 percent higher relative to the Texas average.
- For every ten jobs at Dell Technologies in Texas, another 34 jobs are supported in the state.
- Dell Technologies' operations, supply chain activity, and induced activity produces $95 million in weekly wages in Texas.
- Dell Technologies has a $10 billion annual economic impact on Texas.

Impacting Local Communities

Dell Technologies provides evidence of its commitment to good corporate citizenship in numerous ways. Since 2014, the company has provided five million hours of volunteer time to local communities across the globe. Dell also created a global online portal to better connect team members to local charities' opportunities, and has encouraged skills-based volunteering, from mentoring students to developing new nonprofit technology solutions.

In 2018, Dell provided $68.5 million in cash and in-kind contributions. That same year, the company matched $9.1 million in team member donations through Dell's global matching gifts program – up to $10,000 per team member per calendar year.

More recently, 52 percent of Dell's team members in 2019 registered at least one volunteer activity through the company's online tracking system. Those volunteers collectively logged 890,000 hours of service, and their work positively impacted 13,600 charities worldwide, with education and human services being the most popular causes.

Dell's commitment to its employees and their communities has led to awards too numerous to list. Among the most recent are the Forbes 2019 list of "The Best Employers for Diversity"; the Fortune 2019 list of "World's Most Admired Companies"; the Readers' Choice 2019 "Top 50 Employer Award"; the Fast Company 2019 list of "Most Innovative Companies"; and the Ethisphere 2019 list of "World's Most Ethical Companies; among others.

Dell has helped train and support thousands of workers who have gone on to create their own companies in and around the Austin area while also giving back to the local community. Dell Technologies has played a key role in the growth of the tech ecosystem in the Austin area and is excited to see how the city will continue to grow and thrive in the future.

Additionally, Michael and Susan opened the doors of their family foundation, the Michael & Susan Dell Foundation, in 1999 with the mission of transforming the lives of children living in urban poverty through improved education, health, and financial economic stability. To date, the foundation has committed $420 million in Central Texas, and more than $1.7 billion globally to programs designed to accelerate opportunity for children and families. The initiatives of the Dell Foundation have positively impacted millions of underserved families across the world.

Terry Allen, "Road Angel," 2016. Artwork © Terry Allen. Courtesy of The Contemporary Austin - Laguna Gloria

Photo by Noah Towery

Connecting People, Jobs, and Communities

Delivering 30 million rides a year and covering a service area of more than 544 miles, the Austin area's transit authority has its work cut out for it. But the agency considers itself more than a people mover; instead, it seeks to improve the way the city grows, making it easier and more efficient for people from across the region to connect to jobs, healthcare, education and all the places that makes Austin a desirable place to live. The notion that great cities have great transit systems led to the creation of an organization that would be responsible for providing this essential public service to the people of Austin and Central Texas. Established by a referendum of voters in Austin and the surrounding area on January 19, 1985, the Capital Metro Transportation Authority was established to provide quality transportation choices to the people of Central Texas. For more than three decades, it has done exactly that.

More than 1.2 million people in a service area that includes the cities of Austin, Jonestown, Lago Vista, Leander, Manor, Point Venture, and San Leanna, along with other portions of Travis County and Williamson County, are served by the Authority. Employing almost 500 people, Capital Metro delivers $300 million in economic impact to the Central Texas economy by employing administrative and operations staff. Taking transit rather than driving personal vehicles saves Central Texans more than $57 million annually, which in turn is spent in other ways, generating another $68 million in output.

A Focus on the Customer

A quality transportation system brings people together and serves everyone in a community. Strict adherence to the principles on which the agency was founded - safety and customer service - has led Cap Metro to be named by the Texas Transit Association the 2019 "Agency of the Year." The agency also earned the "2019 Bus Safety and Security Gold Award" from the American Public Transportation Association.

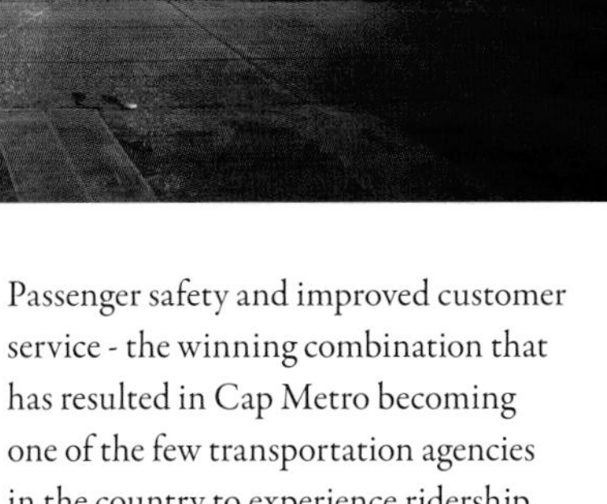

Cap Metro's management team is not content, however, to rest on its laurels. The Central Texas region is rapidly changing. The area's population, which recently hit the two million mark, is projected to double by 2040. Instead of wondering how to fit more cars on the area's roads, Capital Metro is working with the community and partner agencies to figure out how they can join together to move more people more efficiently.

Community outreach efforts indicated that customers wanted transit that is more frequent and more reliable. Project Connect, Cap Metro's regional transportation vision for the future, will deliver a complete system of connected, reliable, and frequent transit services that will improve the quality of life for people in the area. It aims to provide high-capacity transit on several corridors throughout the city and region. That entails transit vehicles traveling in their own dedicated space, free from the flow of traffic, ensuring reliable and frequent service.

Passenger safety and improved customer service - the winning combination that has resulted in Cap Metro becoming one of the few transportation agencies in the country to experience ridership increases in the past half-decade.

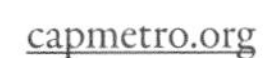

capmetro.org

We Exist to Build Great Things.®

FOUNDED IN 1990, DPR CONSTRUCTION IS A FORWARD-THINKING, SELF-PERFORMING GENERAL CONTRACTOR AND CONSTRUCTION MANAGER WITH AN INTERNATIONAL PRESENCE THAT SPECIALIZES IN TECHNICALLY-COMPLEX AND SUSTAINABLE PROJECTS. FOCUSED ON ADVANCED TECHNOLOGY/MISSION CRITICAL, LIFE SCIENCES, healthcare, higher education, and commercial markets, DPR has been ranked among the top 50 general contractors in the US since 1997. In fact, DPR has consistently ranked first on the *Austin Business Journal*'s Book of Lists for top Austin-area commercial construction companies year after year.

"We are a company of builders building great projects, great teams, great relationships, and great value," stated Peter Nosler, DPR Co-Founder and DPR Foundation Board Member. "We pledge to continue building a great reputation for honoring commitments—doing what is right for employees, customers, our communities, and the industry."

While the privately held, employee-owned company has grown to a multi-billion-dollar organization with offices around the world, you'd never know it. DPR strives to be the best; they're a 'boots on the ground' type of company that enables its employees to make the right decisions in the field. Its local mentality, purpose, and core values are not only evident at each of its locations, they underlie the passion that drives its employees to be better and different. These core values allow the freedoms of its entrepreneurial, innovative organization, where people can make a difference with their ideas and hard work.

Transforming the Live Music Capital of the World

Since establishing its local presence in 1994, DPR has completed numerous ground-up projects, making an eminent impact on Austin's skyline and its surrounding areas of growth. Notable projects include:

- JW Marriott
- Third + Shoal Office Building
- Colorado Tower
- Aloft/Element Hotel
- Block 185
- Charles Schwab Corporate Campus
- Waterloo Park & Amphitheater
- Marriott Austin Downtown
- Block 71
- Domain 11, 12 & Northside
- University of Texas Robert B. Rowling Hall
- University of Texas Systems Building
- The Foundry & Foundry II
- HP Tandem Data Center
- MLS 13 Motorola
- Dell Computer Campus
- University of Texas High Performance Computer Center

Additionally, DPR has completed renovations, expansions, and tenant improvement projects for companies such as Google, VISA, Zynga, Hospital Corporation of America, USAA, St. David's Medical Center, Bank of America, Scott & White, the University of Texas at Austin, Advanced Micro Devices, MTEM, and more.

"Our distinct purpose of building great things and the core values we dialed in on - integrity, enjoyment, uniqueness, ever forward - emulate the way we like to work. And, we like to live and transcend into the way we do business...again, doing something different in an industry that has not always had a reputation for integrity and doing things right the first time," added Ron Davidowski, DPR Co-Founder.

(continued on next page)

1. BLOCK 185
2. THIRD & SHOAL
3. UT ROBERT B. ROWING HALL
4. AUTOGRAPH AC HOTEL
5. BLOCK 71
6. UT SYSTEM BUILDING
7. COLORADO TOWER
8. ALOFT/ELEMENT HOTEL
9. WATERLOO PARK
10. JW MARRIOTT
11. MARRIOTT CESAR CHAVEZ
12. THE FOUNDRY (BLDG 1 & 2)

Image (left): Located in the heart of the East Side, DPR's Austin office features a gallery wall of DPR's self-performed trades and installations by local artists capturing the spirit of Austin. Image (above): Building great things in the Lone Star State since 1994, DPR has constructed major projects that have transformed the downtown Austin skyline.

Investing in the Community

Beyond building projects, DPR is committed to being integral and indispensable to the communities in which it serves. Whether employees are supporting an under-resourced community, donating monetarily, or fulfilling skills-based volunteering needs, DPR leverages its unique professional capabilities and resources to make the greatest impact. Much like the disciplined approach it takes to win work and build great buildings, DPR is disciplined and purposeful in terms of how it focuses its philanthropic efforts. In fact, the company identified three key areas in which its skills and expertise most closely align with the needs of local communities. Also known as the Three Pillars, these areas include: Facility Construction & Renovation, Career & Education Guidance for Youth, and Operational Support for Nonprofit Partners.

In Austin, DPR works most closely with LifeWorks, Community First! Village, Austin Sunshine Camps, the Ronald McDonald House Charities of Central Texas, The American Heart Association, GEN Austin, and Girlstart. In 2019, the Association of Fundraising Professionals honored DPR as its "2019 Outstanding Philanthropic Small or Medium Corporation."

Images (left): DPR has partnered with Austin-based nonprofits such as Girlstart to expose local youth to career paths in construction and offer education guidance. Images (above and below): DPR's office, located on the East side, reflects both DPR's operational approach and culture. Featuring elements and materials familiar to jobsites, prominent skylights, a living green wall, an open floor plan, technology-enabled conference rooms, an innovation lab, a gallery wall that depicts DPR's self-performed trades, installations by local artists, and several areas dedicated specifically to employee enjoyment, the space seamlessly balances work, play and the spirit of Austin.

Austin Convention Center

Proudly Serving the City of Austin

IN THE LATTER YEARS OF THE TWENTIETH CENTURY, AUSTIN WAS BECOMING KNOWN AS A CITY RAPIDLY EMERGING AS A GREAT PLACE TO LIVE AND A POWERFUL MAGNET FOR TOURISTS AND CONVENTIONS. BY 1990, IT HAD BECOME EVIDENT TO CITY LEADERS THAT THE CITY WAS MISSING A KEY PIECE OF INFRASTRUCTURE TO host about half a million guests throughout the year. Those leaders sought to alleviate the problem with the creation of a world-class meeting and convention complex that would provide outstanding event facilities and services for attendees of meetings, conventions, and public consumer shows.

The result was the opening in 1992 of the Neal Kocurek Memorial Austin Convention Center, serving as an economic engine for the city of Austin..

The accolades were quick to appear. In 2016, Forbes ranked Austin Number One on its "Cities of the Future" list. U.S. News & World Report named Austin the Number One place to live in the U.S. for 2017 and 2018.

The Shining Star of the Lone Star State

The Austin Convention Center (ACC) is a USGBC LEED® Gold EB certified venue located in the heart of Austin. The facility's convenient location on East Cesar Chavez Street in the heart of downtown Austin provides easy access to the Austin-Bergstrom International Airport, I-35, or Loop 1 by car or public transportation.

Stretching over six city blocks, the Convention Center offers meeting and convention planners 374,278 gross square feet of quality meeting and exhibit space. The facility's five contiguous exhibit halls offer 247,052 square feet of column-free space.

The Convention Center is also centrally located to upwards of 11,000 guest rooms in hotels within a two-mile radius. By the end of 2020, it is estimated that the number of hotel rooms will increase to more than 12,000.

The ACC team is also proud of their efforts in positively impacting the community through several "green-oriented" initiatives. The facility is powered by 100 percent renewable energy from Austin Energy's Green Choice Program. In addition, 50 percent of all waste generated is diverted from landfills through the ACC's extensive recycling, reuse, and composting program.

The Venue of Choice

The ACC's world-class facilities provided and the efforts of its almost 500 full and part-time staff have produced dramatic results. Results from client surveys received after their events consistently demonstrate the ACC's commitment to delivering outstanding services and facilities enabling clients to have a positive experience.

Cindy Jackson, Associate Executive Director of the Texas Association of Secondary School Principals (TASSP), weighed in on their 2018 Summer Workshop. "Our members love coming to Austin! They attend professional development sessions all day, and, in the eventing, they take advantage of the diverse entertainment and cuisine options in downtown Austin. There are activities for families which include museums, movies, shopping, exercising, and more. For the athletic enthusiast, there are plenty of trails to follow. For those interested in cultural events, they find adventure in Austin."

Visit Austin!

Heart and Soul of Austin

GREAT DOWNTOWNS DON'T JUST HAPPEN. THEY ARE BUILT BY PEOPLE AND ORGANIZATIONS THAT CARE DEEPLY ABOUT MAKING THE DOWNTOWN AREA WELCOMING, VIBRANT, AND VITALLY IMPORTANT TO THE CULTURE OF THE CITY AT LARGE.

The Downtown Austin Alliance was incorporated in May 1992 to do exactly that. The following year, the Austin City Council created a Public Improvement District (PID) to provide constant and permanent funding to implement downtown initiatives. Roughly bounded by Martin Luther King Blvd. to the north, Riverside Dr. to the south, IH-35 Access Rd. to the east and San Antonio St. to the west, the PID is a means for the downtown property owners to provide adequate and constant funds for supplemental direct services, projects, signature events and activations, and planning for the future of downtown Austin.

A Vision For Austin

The 25 dedicated employees of the Downtown Alliance are passionate about helping make Austin the absolute best version of itself. They work closely with other city and community entities to guide and shape the city's growth in a way that is responsible to current and future Austinites. The team's deliberate planning, urban design expertise, and enthusiastic collaboration address both present needs and their hope for the future.

The Downtown Alliance enjoys the unique opportunity to work closely with the City of Austin, downtown property owners, and the community to create, preserve and enhance the value and vitality of downtown Austin.

Signature Projects

The Downtown Austin Alliance devotes its vision and voice to an array of programs, projects, and issues that promote, protect, and advocate for downtown Austin. Among the Downtown Alliance's most visible success stories is the revitalization of Republic Square. Through a unique public-private partnership, the Downtown Austin Alliance, Austin Parks Foundation, and the City of Austin Parks and Recreation Department renovated Republic Square and elevated its status once again as an important gathering place in the heart of downtown Austin. Since 2017, the Downtown Alliance has operated and programmed the park, averaging over 100 days of free programs and events for the public.

In addition, the Downtown Alliance is proud to be one of the founding entities of the Innovation District—a place where innovators, incubators, and businesses co-locate and discover new ways to build inclusive economic growth.

The Downtown Alliance team also developed the first-ever comprehensive inventory of downtown parking spaces which led to the formulation of 19 short- and long-term improvement strategies. They continue working to implement these strategies through partnerships and programs such as the Affordable Parking Program.

"Our work helps make Austin the most dynamic city in the country," states Dewitt Peart, the Downtown Alliance President and CEO. "Downtown is not only the economic engine of the region, but is also the heart and soul of the city. The Downtown Alliance's projects, programs, and planning are guided by a commitment to making sure that downtown Austin is—and remains—an incredible place to live, work, and play."

Photo by Michael Knox

Photo by Michael Knox

Photo by Dana Hansen

LUMINEX CORPORATION

From Humble Beginnings to Advancing Health

WHO COULD HAVE GUESSED THAT AN AUSTIN-BASED COMPANY RECOGNIZED BY FORBES MAGAZINE AS ONE OF THE 25 FASTEST GROWING TECHNOLOGY COMPANIES IN THE U.S. THREE YEARS IN A ROW HAD ITS BEGINNINGS SKETCHED ON A COCKTAIL NAPKIN IN A DALLAS RESTAURANT IN 1994?

This is how Luminex began—it started with a group of interdisciplinary scientists who came together to discuss an idea and went on to develop a strategy for measuring multiple biomolecules in biological samples.

Luminex has come a long way since then. While the company was not the first to use colored beads in flow cytometry applications, its approach was innovative, and proved to be a huge success as Luminex's xMAP® Microspheres have delivered reliable and reproducible results over the past three decades—due, in large part, to intelligent design and stringent manufacturing procedures.

BUILDING AUSTIN'S BIOTECHNOLOGY COMMUNITY

Today, Luminex works to empower labs to obtain reliable, timely, and actionable answers, ultimately advancing health. Luminex offers a broad range of solutions applicable to diverse markets, including clinical diagnostics, pharmaceutical drug discovery, biomedical research, genomic and proteomic research, biodefense research, and food safety. Luminex technology enables clinicians and researchers to identify genetic and infectious diseases, develop new medical therapies, and deliver faster, more targeted patient outcomes.

Luminex's corporate headquarters are on a sprawling campus in North Austin. From here, the company coordinates its global operations through offices in Beijing, Chicago, Hong Kong, Madison, the Netherlands, Seattle, Shanghai, Tokyo, and Toronto. Additional functions in Austin include Customer Support, Finance, Human Resources, I.T., Legal, Marketing, Research and Development, Sales Operations, and Training. Additionally, Luminex is proud to manufacture the majority of its products here in Austin.

While most of the biotechnology hubs are located on either coast (in Boston, San Diego, and San Francisco), Luminex has demonstrated a commitment to Austin by continually recruiting professionals to our wonderful city. This commitment has made Luminex the largest biotechnology employer based in Austin.

A TECHNOLOGY LEADER

Luminex technologies power a broad range of molecular diagnostic tests

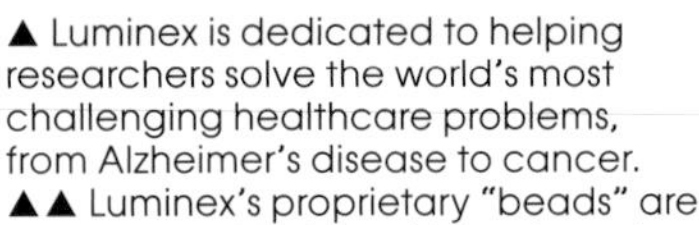

▲ Luminex is dedicated to helping researchers solve the world's most challenging healthcare problems, from Alzheimer's disease to cancer.
▲▲ Luminex's proprietary "beads" are used worldwide in a wide variety of applications, from clinical diagnostics and pharmaceutical drug discovery, to biomedical research, genomic and proteomic research, biodefense research, and food safety.

that help clinicians make critical patient-treatment decisions. Its partner companies use xMAP Technology as the foundation for diagnostic tests of their own design. Through its unique "multiplexing" capability—the ability to measure multiple targets in a single sample—xMAP allows users to collect large amounts of data in one test, rather than having to perform several separate tests. This approach reduces time to answers, lowers laboratory costs, and minimizes the possibility of human error.

Luminex has expanded from its multiplexing foundation into sample to answer instruments and diagnostic tests for use in clinical laboratories and hospitals. The company now offers a broad range of solutions for all levels of laboratory throughput. By integrating cell analyzers and flow cytometers into its technology portfolio, Luminex has options available for startup labs, research labs, reference labs, and even pharmaceutical companies—flexibility is a cornerstone of Luminex's commitment to providing solutions for every lab's needs.

Since its historic initial lunch, Luminex has become recognized as the worldwide leader in bead-based multiplexing, with its xMAP Technology featured in more than 46,000 scientific publications.

Luminex has also received numerous industry awards due to its innovative developments, including:

- 2010 – Prix Galien USA Award for best medical technology (xTAG® Respiratory Viral Panel Assay)
- 2011 – Medical Design Excellence Award for MAGPIX® multiplexing bioassay platform
- 2011 – Deloitte Technology Fast 500, Deloitte
- 2011 – Top 25 Fastest Growing Technology Companies, Forbes
- 2012 – Best Technology Company in Austin, Austin Chamber of Commerce
- 2016 – R&D 100 Awards Winner for the ARIES® System, R&D Conference
- 2018 – MedTech Regulatory Award from the Arazy Group

Commitment to Austin

Along the way, Luminex has been recognized by the mayor of Austin as a Mother Friendly Workplace, and with its 500 local employees, won the Most Fit Company in Austin award two years in a row. Through the company's Employee Community Involvement Committee, Luminex supports programs like Be-The-Match, "Great Strides" for Cystic Fibrosis, the Sepsis Alliance, "Souls 4 Soles," the Dell Children's Medical Center of Texas, and the Cure for Alzheimer's.

Additionally, members of the Luminex team hold leadership roles in BioAustin, the Austin Chamber of Commerce, the Austin Technology Council, the Austin Regional Manufacturing Association, and Workforce Solutions—all organizations focused on advancing the growth, development, and well-being of the Austin business community.

The Luminex management team recognizes the abundance of biomedical talent in Texas, and its Austin headquarters is truly a beacon for igniting innovation and creativity. For 25 years, Luminex has developed and led the local biotechnology community, contributing to Austin's robust economic growth by creating high-paying jobs and bringing the best and brightest talent from across the globe. With humble beginnings and a strong foundation, Luminex is looking forward to many years of growth to come in our wonderful home town of Austin, Texas.

▲ Founded in 1995, Luminex is the largest biotech company headquartered in Austin. The company is striving to transform global healthcare by developing and manufacturing innovative products that empower laboratories to obtain reliable, timely, and actionable answers.

▼ Luminex is at the leading edge of infectious disease testing, developing solutions to improve how physicians make treatment decisions for patients while reducing overall cost to the healthcare system.

Offering Award-Winning Solutions for More Than Two Decades

Since 1996, SKG has been successfully transforming traditional workspace systems into environments connecting people to productivity, talent to brand and vision, and individual lives to commitment. During that time, SKG has become the exclusive distributor of Knoll products for Austin, San Antonio, and Central and South Texas. The company today is one of the largest Knoll dealerships in the country and the second largest woman-owned business in Central Texas. Its impressive portfolio of projects spans the country and includes corporate, government, education, and healthcare environments.

▲ SKG was instrumental in the repurposing of the Holy Cross building on the campus of St. Edward's University.

▲ At the SKG showroom the latest styles are shown along with the timeless designs of their flagship brand, Knoll.

In addition to being the authorized Knoll dealership in Central and South Texas, SKG is currently working on projects nationally. The company has successfully completed projects on the East and West Coasts of the U.S. as well as in Barbados and Canada.

▼ SKG provides furniture solutions from the boardroom to the breakroom, like here at the headquarters of uShip.

Roots in the Lone Star State

Ron Shelton was working for a Knoll dealership in Dallas in the mid-1990s when Knoll approached him on the company's idea of expanding its distribution network in Austin. Ron asked Diana Keller if she would be interested in joining him in a business partnership that would do just that. She gave an enthusiastic thumbs-up on the idea.

"We were excited about the possibility of exploiting an underserved market," Diana recalls. "I loved the idea of a start-up," she adds, "of getting things started from nothing."

After spending a year formulating their business plan and being turned down by five banks on financing, the sixth bank they approached said "yes." SKG was incorporated as the Shelton-Keller Group in October 1995 and opened its doors in downtown Austin in January of the following year.

The bank that took a chance on them remains their business partner a quarter century later.

A Record of Success

While Shelton retired from the business in 2015, Diana continues to serve as SKG's President. She also forged a new partnership with Beth Goff-McMillan. Under their watch, the company has expanded dramatically. More than 80 design, support, and strategic workplace SKG professionals serve clients across the country.

In addition to its Austin headquarters, with its 10,000 square feet of office space, 25,000-square-foot showroom, and an auxiliary warehouse for showroom management, SKG now includes a second location in San Antonio. A third location is planned for College Station along with an e-commerce site.

"Diana has fostered the company's growth with an impeccable record of customer service," notes McMillan, the company's CEO. "As a devotee of design with an ability to understand the subtle functional elements most people take for granted in their daily lives, she has instilled in the organization a focus on achieving a successful outcome for every client."

McMillan's new vision for the company, which focuses on strategic space planning, is a disruptive concept at home in a market full of entrepreneurs disrupting their industries on a daily basis. To change the experience, SKG has had to change its approach, its staff, its technology, products, and services.

"SKG's mission is to provide the 'Spaces to Live the Life of Your Business'," McMillan adds. "Most businesses in our industry are focused solely on selling furniture. We learn how each of our customers will use the space they plan to occupy so we can offer the right combination of furniture, architectural and technology solutions to create the ideal working, learning, healing or hospitality environment."

Setting the Standard

SKG has been the company that some of the most recognized names in the region and across the country have turned to with confidence. The company's professionals furnished the local headquarters of the world's largest Internet services company; Texas A&M University (1.8 million square feet); the City of Austin; Bergstrom International Airport; Kendra Scott; and E-Trade, among others.

SKG's phenomenal success story across many fronts has not gone unnoticed, both in the Austin area and around the country. The company is ranked Number One on the *Austin Business Journal*'s most recent list of largest commercial furniture dealers. In 2019, SKG jumped 1,700 spots on the *Inc.* 5000 list of largest private companies and made its second appearance on the *ABJ*'s Fast 50 list of fastest growing companies. Other awards include *Austin American-Statesman* Top Workplace in 2018; *ABJ*'s Top Private Company in 2017; and the *ABJ*'s Top Women-Owned Business for three consecutive years beginning in 2015.

With women in the top management positions at SKG, the company has maintained an unwavering focus on women's issues. SKG actively supports the Austin Community Foundation, the Austin Women's Fund, Salvation Army, the Refuge, and Austin Diaper Bank.

"What began as a furniture dealer has evolved today into a business focused on helping organizations think strategically," McMillan points out. "Our industry - commercial furniture manufacturing - has traditionally been a male-dominated space. We have hired a lot of women, not all of them with design and furniture backgrounds, and created a diverse and empowered workforce. We have created an environment that offers the support and flexibility for people with families that we never had when we were working for other people all while disrupting our market and changing our industry."

▲ SKG furnished the headquarters of The Chive, called the "coolest office" in Austin by a local business publication.

▼ The Kendra Scott conference room provides another opportunity for SKG Inc. to reinforce the Kendra Scott brand.

Marketing Austin to the World

SINCE 1996, VISIT AUSTIN HAS BEEN ENRICHING THE QUALITY OF LIFE FOR THE AUSTIN COMMUNITY BY MARKETING THE CITY AS A PREMIERE DESTINATION FOR VISITORS AND AS A WORLD-CLASS VENUE FOR BUSINESS TRAVEL. THE ORGANIZATION, A PRIVATE, NON-PROFIT 501(C)6 CORPORATION, OPERATES INDEPENDENTLY and is contracted by the city to promote Austin as a city replete with history and a rich tapestry of cultures that attracts visitors from around the globe. In addition, Visit Austin operates the Austin Visitor Center and houses the Austin Film Commission, Austin Music Office, Austin Sports Commission, and Visit Austin Foundation.

Photo courtesy of Visit Austin

The more than 60 full-time and part-time Visit Austin team members are constantly adapting their approach to solidify Austin's position as a premier leisure, convention, and meetings destination. Connecting with Visit Austin ensures working with a group of passionate locals who have made a career out of their love for the city. From the organization's Convention Sales and Services teams, to the staff at the Austin Visitor Center and everyone in between, Visit Austin professionals focus on exceeding expectations and making each experience in Austin everything it ought to be.

The organization's Sales staff works to book and promote group business for both the Austin Convention Center and the hotel community. Actively highlighting the local business community, the Sales and Services teams encourage clients to incorporate uniquely Austin themes into conference programming, which always contributes to added attendee excitement when visiting Austin.

AN IMPRESSIVE SPOTLIGHT

The City of Austin has much to offer. Austin is served by Austin-Bergstrom International Airport, the second fastest growing midsize airport in the United States and recognized as the "2017 Airport of the Year" by the Airline Pilots Association. The almost 16 million passengers who filed through the airport in 2018 were taking advantage of Austin-Bergstrom's more than 70 nonstop destinations across North America and Europe.

The city's emerging tech market and expanding economy have led to increased awareness and excitement surrounding Austin as a hot destination, boosting tourism in both the leisure and meetings sectors. Meeting planners have discovered the recent boom in hotel inventory growth, with a projected 12,700 rooms downtown and 44,427 rooms citywide by 2020. This will culminate in a more than 96 percent projected increase in the downtown sector from 2014-2020 and a more than 42 percent increase citywide, during the same period. The Convention Sales & Services teams offer personalized sales assistance for groups needing ten or more rooms, helping clients with everything from checking hotel availability to planning and site visit assistance to ensure groups execute successful events in Austin.

Leisure travelers are discovering Austin's abundant attractions as well. Austin is not only the capital of Texas, the city is also the home of the University of Texas at Austin® and gateway to the beautiful Hill Country. As the Live Music Capital of the World®, the city has a soundtrack all its own. More than 250 live music venues flourish with rock, indie, hip hop, Tejano, and more. Visit Austin reinforces this brand positioning through a variety of strategic sales and marketing tactics.

Top-notch restaurants whet visitors' appetites with legendary barbecue and farm-to-table cuisine. Shoppers find trea-

Photo by Nick Simonite, courtesy of Visit Austin

Photo by Roger Ho, courtesy of Visit Austin

sures in the one-of-a-kind boutiques that line the city's streets and neighborhoods. Others head out to the Hill Country to relax in a world-class destination spa.

A Strong Community Partner

Visit Austin serves as an economic engine for the City of Austin, aiming to support and promote Austin's community through its various activities. The Austin Film Commission supports Austin's growing film industry, while maintaining a strong relationship with the local film community. The Austin Music Office recommends local bands and musicians for conventions and corporate meetings, thereby actively working to get musicians hired.

In 2019, Visit Austin launched the Visit Austin Foundation. The Foundation's mission is to develop and promote education, job training, and career opportunities within the hospitality, music, and tourism community in the greater Austin area. The tourism and hospitality industry is one of the top employers in the city annually, contributing to a large tax savings for residents each year. Visit Austin and the Visit Austin Foundation host the annual Tourism & Hospitality Career Fair, which aims to introduce those looking to start or grow their careers in the industry by promoting positions from entry level to management.

A Partnership for the Future

The success of Visit Austin's efforts to spotlight the Capital City are evident in numerous ways. Austin is the recipient of the J.D. Power and Associates 2016 Destination Experience Satisfaction Award. That same year, Austin was ranked Number One in the Southwest U.S. and Number Two overall in the country.

Other accolades arrived in 2018 as Austin ranked Number Four in Expedia's "Most Tourist Friendly Cities in the U.S." and industry buzz ranked Austin Number One among cities in the U.S. and Canada for providing the most positive overall experience for major conventions.

More recently, in June 2019 Travel & Leisure Magazine named Austin Number 13 in their list of "Top 15 Cities in the United States."

"Austin continues to grow larger and more diverse," states Tom Noonan, Visit Austin President and CEO. "We are a city built on cultivating new ideas with a community of residents that continue to roll out the red carpet for visitors from all over the world. At Visit Austin, we are proud to be a part of the hospitality community, the industry that is the front door to our community letting the world know, 'You're invited'."

Photo by Nick Simonite, courtesy of Visit Austin

Photo by Jody Horton Photography, courtesy of Visit Austin

Photo by Geoff Duncan, courtesy of Visit Austin

Growing Together With Austin

IN 1998, SEVEN ENTREPRENEURIAL TEXANS FOUNDED TEXAS CAPITAL BANK ON THE VISION OF PROVIDING SMALL AND MID-SIZED BUSINESSES WITH RELATIONSHIP-DRIVEN, SOLUTIONS-BASED BANKING. BY 2000, TEXAS CAPITAL BANK HAD FILLED AN IMPORTANT NICHE IN THE MARKET – TEXAS BUSINESS OWNERS WERE KEEN TO bank with top-notch professionals who knew the fine points of their industries. Austin became the bank's third market location.

"Each city in which we set out to launch our business has special qualities," says Keith Cargill, Texas Capital Bank President and CEO. "In Austin, we saw the opportunity to grow something unique, but also to create something complementary to the special personality and aspirations of the city."

The bank's leadership believed that attracting the best talent and providing a differentiated client experience was the right path forward. They saw the chance for their bank to play a role in growing one of the greatest cities in the country.

▼ Texas Business Hall of Fame Induction Kick-Off 2019. (Left to right: Chris Calvert, Vera Gebert, Kendra Scott [inductee], Robert Smith [inductee], Jennifer Guthrie, and Mike McConnell.)
▼▼ Highland Resources, Inc.'s 160,000-square-foot building at 38th Street and Lamar Boulevard.

Photo courtesy of Highland Resources, Inc.

A PREMIER CLIENT EXPERIENCE

In Austin, Texas Capital Bank started from scratch with just five employees. Kerry Hall, now Executive Managing Director, Regional and Commercial Banking, helped build the bank from a makeshift office in her kitchen.

"From the beginning, our unique differentiation in the market has rested on our commitment to providing service that draws on deep industry knowledge, experience, and connections," Kerry says. "We've grown alongside some of Austin's most influential entrepreneurs, and it's because of them that we've grown to be the sixth-largest bank in terms of deposits in just 20 years."

One of the bank's first Austin clients was ABC Home & Commercial Services. In 2000, the company employed 218 people; today, ABC has 820 employees spread across Central Texas. Bobby Jenkins, ABC's majority owner, is a member of Texas Capital Bank's Austin Advisory Board, which brings together local leaders who offer the bank advice and support.

When Trinity Episcopal School became a Texas Capital Bank client, it had 103 students; now, more than 540 are enrolled. Trinity Episcopal School's infrastructure comprises 100,000 square feet of buildings at its beautiful West Lake Hills campus.

In 2005, Brian Pitman and Jay Southworth left their positions at major title companies to start Independence Title Company, which launched as a client of Texas Capital Bank. Currently Independence employs about 500 people and is licensed in more than 40 counties.

Kendra Scott came to Texas Capital Bank in 2007, when her jewelry company was wholesale only. Today the brand is an omnichannel retailer that employs 2,000 people and encompasses nearly 100 standalone stores. Kendra remains one of the bank's most vocal supporters, and in 2019, she joined the Austin Advisory Board. Kendra was inducted into the Texas Business Hall of Fame in October 2019.

Providing a premier client experience means facilitating clients' growth but also being there for them when they experience a life-changing liquidity event. In 2014, Texas Capital Bank introduced its private wealth advisory services to Austin, enabling the bank to help high-net-worth clients with their financial needs for decades to come.

A Leader in the Community

In 2004, Texas Capital Bank linked arms with the Greater Austin Chamber of Commerce to support Opportunity Austin, an initiative focused on economic development for the region. The initiative, and the supporters who launched it, helped spur an era of prosperity – and Texas Capital Bank has never wavered from its commitment to the community.

Between 2016 and 2018, the bank's Austin location approved more than $128 million in loans and investments toward community development. The bank contributed nearly $450,000 in community development grants, and employees donated more than 2,000 community service hours. The bank supports Community First! Village, Caritas, and Texas State Affordable Housing Corporation, among other organizations that deal with affordability and homelessness issues.

In 2015, bank employees formed the Employee Engagement Committee, through which Texas Capital Bank assists Martin Middle School, Meals on Wheels Central Texas, Junior Achievement, and the Central Texas Food Bank.

Proud to Be Part of Austin's Story

Texas Capital Bank's success is intertwined with its clients' accomplishments – and sometimes, this collective impact is visible in Austin's landscape. In 2014, the bank's Commercial Real Estate team financed the construction of a 160,000-square-foot, class-A office building for Highland Resources, Inc. The building is located at 38th Street and Lamar Boulevard, and Kendra Scott is the lead tenant. Texas Capital Bank is also the financial force behind the Met Center, longtime client Howard Yancy's sprawling industrial campus.

Texas Capital Bank started in Austin 20 years ago. Today, the bank employs 50 people and is located in downtown Austin, not far from the sparkling waters of Lady Bird Lake.

"Our growth is a reflection of the clients we attract, of their growth, and of how we've helped them achieve it," says Chris Calvert, President, Texas Capital Bank Austin Region. "Today, Austin is one of the most vibrant, well-educated, innovative economies in the country. We're proud to have grown deep roots in this dynamic city, and we're excited for what's to come."

▲ On Texas Capital Bank's Day of Caring, employees provided more than 20,000 meals for Meals on Wheels recipients statewide.

▶ Texas Capital Bank Mobile Center. (Left to right: Christopher Rios; Ashton Cumberbatch, President, Equidad, ATX; Kerry Hall; and Derrick Chubbs, President/CEO Central Texas Food Bank.)

▶ The team that has fun together stays together. (Left to right: Chris Wheeler, who's been with the bank for 18 years; Doug Cotner, 15 years; and Chris Calvert, 19 years.)

▼ Celebrating 20 years in Austin.

Austin's Front Door

Almost 16 million passengers traveled through Austin-Bergstrom International Airport (AUS) in 2018. Those travelers took advantage of the more than 70 destinations across North America and Europe that are accessible through what has become the airport of choice for passengers in Central Texas.

Owned by the City of Austin and operated by the Department of Aviation, AUS has experienced a phenomenal rate of growth with passenger traffic having grown by an average annual rate of 5.6 percent since 2008 and almost doubling to 9.4 percent since 2013.

With several international nonstop flights and many domestic ones, AUS is Austin's front door. The Austin airport is located in the Capital city of Texas and inside the Metro Triangle (80 percent of Texas' population lives within the triangle of Dallas, San Antonio, and Houston).

AUS is the fourth largest airport in Texas and the second fastest growing mid-sized airport in the United States. Conveniently located just eight miles from downtown Austin, AUS sits on 4,242 acres of land with two all-weather runways that are 12,500 and 9,000 feet in length. The airport consists of two terminals: the Barbara Jordan Terminal with 34 aircraft gates and the South Terminal with three gates. The campus also includes over 15,000 parking spaces, three FBO general aviation facilities, three helipads, and a 27-acre cargo facility.

The City of Austin's Department of Aviation employs 535 total employees as well as ten part-time employees and summer interns. According to the latest TxDOT (Texas Department of Transportation) study, AUS generates 74,000 total jobs and has a $7.6 billion economic impact in the Austin area.

In addition, AUS supports over 60 Honor Flight Austin programs that take veterans from the Austin area to their national monuments in Washington D.C. AUS also supports its neighborhood Del Valle Independent School District by providing mentors for students, school supplies and backpacks, clothing drives, and "Adopt a Family" programs for holidays. The

—Photo by Austin Pro Photo

—Photo by Austin Pro Photo

—Photo by Sandy L. Stevens

airport proudly participates in a Food Rescue Program that collects unsold, packaged fresh food and delivers it to individuals and families via Keep Austin Fed.

A Proud Past

On May 23, 1999, what had been the Robert Mueller Municipal Airport for 60 years officially became the Austin-Bergstrom International Airport. Named after Captain John August Earl Bergstrom, the first native Austinite killed in action during World War II, the airport is built on the location of the former Bergstrom Air Force Base. The airport's subsequent renaming in 1999 capped the development of the AUS of today.

Even though the City of Austin owns the facility, the people and businesses that use the airport pay the entire ongoing budget. Any revenue generated from the airport goes back into its operations, covering its operating expenses.

An Exciting Future

Central Texas depends on reliable and extensive air service to foster business and leisure opportunities as well as to connect friends and families. To keep up with passenger demand and prepare for future growth, AUS is tuning up with numerous terminal, airfield, and parking service expansions. In 2019, the airport opened its nine-gate expansion of the Barbara Jordan Terminal. This expansion includes highlights such as a new outdoor observation deck, local retail and concession amenities, pet relief area, mothers' lounge, and companion care restroom for adults with varying needs. The South Terminal, home to Allegiant and Frontier, serviced 391,876 passengers in its first complete year of operation in 2018.

Austin is the home of several major events such as Formula 1, Austin City Limit Music Festival, SXSW, and the Austin Film Festival that draws visitors from around the globe. Austin is known as the "Live Music Capitol of the World," and the airport reflects the city's musical heartbeat by providing over 1,190 live music performances per year on six different stages inside the airport. AUS further enhances the city's image with local food, culture, and retail outlets. The airport's stunning art displays reflect Austin's welcoming attitude to visitors attending any of the city's festivals, embracing technology development, and business growth.

In 2017 the Airline Pilots Association recognized AUS with its National Safety Award as "2017 Airport of the Year" for its continued collaboration in partnering with pilots on important safety and construction issues. In addition, Fodor's Travel Awards in 2019 designated AUS as "Runner-up for Best Airport in the U.S."

For the ninth consecutive year, passengers at the Austin-Bergstrom International Airport have set a new annual record as demand for air travel increased to 15.8 million passengers in 2018. That same year, records again increased at AUS as 11 carriers announced or started 42 new routes at the airport.

"The size and growth opportunity at the Austin airport is wonderful," said Jacqueline Yaft, Executive Director, Austin-Bergstrom International Airport. "With all the different destinations, we have the opportunity to provide services from the curb to the sky to the citizens of one of the greatest cities and regions in the U.S."

—Photo by Austin Pro Photo

—Photo by Austin Pro Photo

—Photo by Dave Wilson

Gottesman Residential Real Estate

Setting the Standard for Luxury Real Estate in Austin

Founded in Austin in 2000, Gottesman Residential Real Estate is a progressive and unique boutique brokerage focused on delivering unmatched professionalism to its clients. The firm specializes in Austin's luxury real estate market. The agents pride themselves on the connections they develop with their clients, and aim to extend every transaction into an ongoing relationship in which the entire company becomes a valued resource. Their goal is to exceed every client's expectations.

A New Era in Real Estate

Born and raised in Dallas, Laura Gottesman married her childhood sweetheart (met Morris at age 12!) and made Austin their home. After their three sons were all in school, Laura decided she wanted to focus her energy on residential real estate. To prepare, Laura enrolled in the Business Foundations Program at The University of Texas and took computer classes at Austin Community College.

The real estate community was not tech savvy at that time and was just transitioning into the computer age. Laura was fortunate to start her business with a great network, newly honed technology skills, and a creative and savvy business mentality. Her timing was perfect. She was extremely successful in relocation as Austin was evolving into a tech hub. Work with Dell, Trilogy and Austin Ventures on their executive relocation created a path for Laura to specialize in luxury properties.

Constantly setting higher goals, she began thinking outside of the traditional box. In 2000, she partnered with friend

and fellow Realtor, Shannon Windham, to start their own boutique brokerage company. They specialized in relocation, buyer representation, and a unique approach to marketing listings.

"We recognized an opportunity to make our company a true resource to our clients through our deep knowledge of the community, local connections, and unbeatable service," Laura explains. "With my background in advertising and Shannon's background in design, we created a non-traditional approach to marketing properties which raised the bar for the industry."

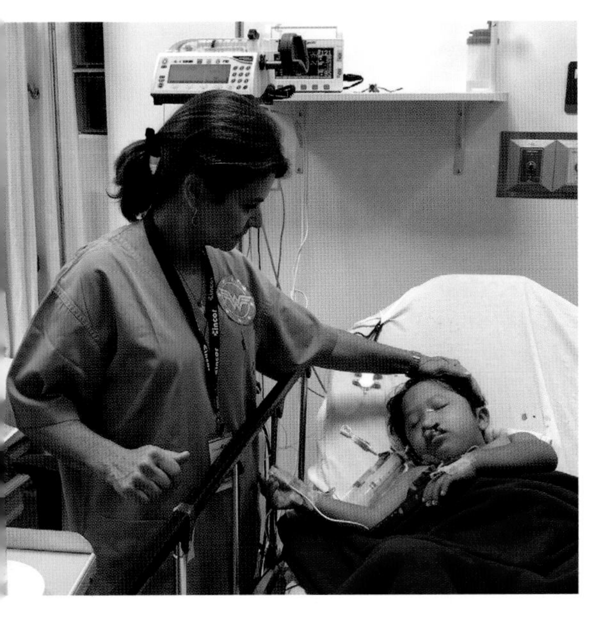

Trust. Integrity. Professionalism.

The Gottesman Residential team enjoys living the motto - "When you get one of us, you get all of us." Trust, Integrity, and Professionalism are the core values.

Since embarking on her chosen road almost two decades ago, Laura has never lost sight of the premise on which she began - to focus on quality over quantity. She is very selective in choosing the right people to join her brokerage. To ensure a collaborative environment, the chemistry, camaraderie, and culture within the office remain paramount.

That selection process and the professional growth it fosters has yielded positive results. Several of the agents who joined the firm as licensed assistants to more seasoned agents have gone on to become top performing agents themselves.

"I have always believed in surrounding myself with greatness," she states. "The agents I work with are the best in the business. We are constantly learning from each other and are better agents because of it."

Gottesman Residential's office is located in a stunning home built in 1927 in Central Austin. Previously the home of the Austin Children's Shelter, Laura purchased and restored the property making it a warm and inviting office in which all of the agents enjoy working. "We sell homes," Laura notes, "so it is wonderful to work out of one and have familial energy in the office."

The company has been continually recognized in the Top 10 Woman Owned Businesses by the Austin Business Journal. Six of the agents are in the prestigious "Elite 25 Austin" and five in the "Luxury League Austin." Throughout Austin, Gottesman Residential and its agents are recognized as leaders in the industry as well as pillars in the community.

Business and Pleasure

After 34 years of marriage, launching and operating a successful boutique real estate business, and watching their sons become successful themselves, Laura and her husband continue to find time to enjoy the fruits of their labors. They remain avid adventure travelers, exploring new cultures and landscapes all over the world. They also love spending time hiking, biking, and snowboarding in Colorado with their family and friends.

Laura is deeply involved in Austin's business and civic community. She manages the Austin Luxury Network; serves on the boards of Elite 25, Greater Austin Economic Development Board, and Executive Advisory Board for Go Red for Women; and is a member of the Founder's Circle of Austin 100.

Another focus of Gottesman Residential is to give back to the community. The brokerage donates the equivalent of 50 percent of the company's net profits to Austin-based charities. In 2019, the firm and its agents set aside a portion of their commissions to underwrite a mission trip for HeartGift, an organization founded in 2001 in Austin that provides life-saving heart surgeries to children around the world where specialized medical treatment is either scarce or nonexistent. Laura has been involved with Heartgift since the organization's inception and continues to donate much of her time to it.

In addition, all of the realtors, brokers, and assistants at Gottesman Residential Real Estate are committed to the local community, touching over 80 organizations by serving on boards, donating, and volunteering.

Transportation Solutions That Enhance the Quality of Life

SHORTLY AFTER THE NEW MILLENNIUM HAD ARRIVED, IT BECAME EVIDENT THAT THE CENTRAL TEXAS REGION WAS FAST EVOLVING AS ONE OF THE NATION'S STRONGEST ECONOMIES. AUSTIN WAS CONSISTENTLY RANKED AS ONE OF THE BEST PLACES TO LIVE IN THE UNITED STATES. ITS POPULARITY WAS FUELED BY A vibrant economy, great climate, and plentiful amenities and opportunities. The city's ranking in 2018 by Forbes in its list of the top ten fastest growing U.S. cities came as little surprise. With a population expected to reach three million by 2030, local lawmakers were faced with the reality that the Central Texas region would continue to attract large numbers of college graduates, families with children, and others pursuing the prospect of a better future and an improved quality of life.

To plan for the present and future transportation needs of the residents and businesses in the area, the Central Texas Regional Mobility Authority (Mobility Authority, or CTRMA) was established by Travis and Williamson Counties in 2002 as the state's first regional mobility authority. The agency represents the Texas Legislature's vision to allow local communities greater flexibility in meeting their transportation needs. While the founding goal of the CTRMA was to improve the transportation system in Travis and Williamson Counties, it may be expanded as needs warrant to other counties.

An Ongoing Mission

The original mission of the CTRMA founders, set forth almost 20 years ago, remains key to the role the Mobility Authority plays today - to implement innovative, multi-modal transportation solutions that reduce congestion and create transportation choices that enhance

the quality of life and economic vitality in Central Texas. The CTRMA was created by need in the region. While the Mobility Authority was designed to serve Central Texans, its roads both impact and provide access to surrounding counties and communities.

The CTRMA continues to operate today as an independent government agency authorized through state legislation in 2002 to improve the transportation system in Williamson and Travis counties. Founded by and still answering to the Commissioners Courts of both counties, the CTRMA is overseen by a seven-member Board of Directors. The Governor appoints the Chairman, and the Travis and Williamson Counties Commissioners Courts each appoint three members to serve on the Board.

Commitment and Accountability

The Mobility Authority employs a small professional staff of 30 led by Executive Director Mike Heiligenstein, who has been involved with the planning, financing, and construction of infrastructure in Central Texas for almost 40 years. Because of his work with the CTRMA he was elected as President of the International Bridge, Tunnel and Turnpike Association. Private sector contractors with specialized expertise are utilized by the CTRMA to provide staffing support for individual projects.

The Mobility Authority is one of nine regional mobility authorities in Texas. The management team is justifiably proud that the Texas A&M Transportation Institute cited the Central Texas Regional Mobility Authority as the standard for transparency and accountability by which other regional mobility authorities in Texas should strive to follow.

The Mobility Authority continues to evolve with the support and guidance of Travis and Williamson Counties, and in collaboration with regional partners. Amidst a transportation funding crisis, the agency has delivered critically needed infrastructure for Central Texas in an efficient and cost-effective manner. The toll facilities owned and operated by the Mobility Authority provide the traveling public with reliable transportation options that enhance the quality of life and economic vitality.

The emergence of 183A Toll, 290 Toll, 71 Toll Lane, and MoPac Express Lane has laid the foundation for a comprehensive, regional roadway network that will continue to reduce travel and response times and spur economic development while reducing air pollution and fuel consumption. To further expand mobility options for the traveling public, the agency has established a partnership with Capital Metro whereby Express buses operate toll-free in the MoPac Express Lane. This partnership has led to increased ridership and new transit routes across the region, and plans are in development for additional Park & Ride facilities to serve Mobility Authority customers.

In addition, the Mobility Authority has created and nurtured a long list of like-minded, sustainable partnerships that are committed to achieving its mission. From civic groups, non-profits, local businesses, and special interest groups to schools, the CTRMA works closely with the communities it serves.

The Mobility Authority's efforts have been recognized with numerous awards, among the most recent being the WTS Heart of Texas Chapter "Innovative Transportation Solutions Award" in 2018 and, in the same year, the Greater Austin Business Awards: Environmental Champion Award for the agency's efforts to promote sustainability and innovation.

With an eye to the future, the agency is positioned to expand beyond toll roads. Leveraging its ability to deliver such projects in a faster, more cost-effective manner, the CTRMA is developing non-tolled projects for Travis County and is exploring the feasibility of further broadening its portfolio to include additional mobility solutions.

A Relationship With Austin

MG Realty Investments (doing business as Momark Development and Groundwork) has been creating great places to live, work, and play in Austin and surrounding communities for 16 years. Each of Momark's communities is unique—designed to improve the lives of the folks who live and work there, and to enhance the quality of life for the entire neighborhood. From the tallest skyscrapers in Austin, to intimate neighborhood projects, Momark delivers places that are at human scale that serve our residents at all income levels. MG's Groundwork division brings a creative, entrepreneurial approach to assisting landowners envision and create world-class places to live, work, and play.

Every community is designed and developed in collaboration with the city and neighborhoods where we build. The company's success is based on a single, guiding vision: to improve people's lives and to create places that bring people together. Everything is to be considered in achieving that objective. Doing what is right for the city and the region benefits everyone.

A Unique Philosophy and Commitment

MG Realty shares the values that make Austin a unique place to live and work. These values include a commitment to sustainable growth, affordable housing, creative transportation solutions, the environment, hard work, quality, long term relationships, and, above all of these, a commitment to creating community.

The 'success stories' that the company is most proud of are the stories of people who come into a space that it has created, and who then connect to each other in lasting ways. These are stories of couples meeting, of friends gathering, of parents of limited means who have found a better home for their children, of grandparents showing the grandkids a great time, and of newcomers finding a warm

and welcoming environment from which they can explore all that Austin has to offer. All of this seems effortless when one walks into a community designed to change people's lives for the better, but it is far from easy. MG Realty aligns itself with the singular focus of improving people's lives. That mindset results in unique places that enhance the city and work harmoniously with the neighborhood, offering an amenity-rich environment for the people who call the company's projects home.

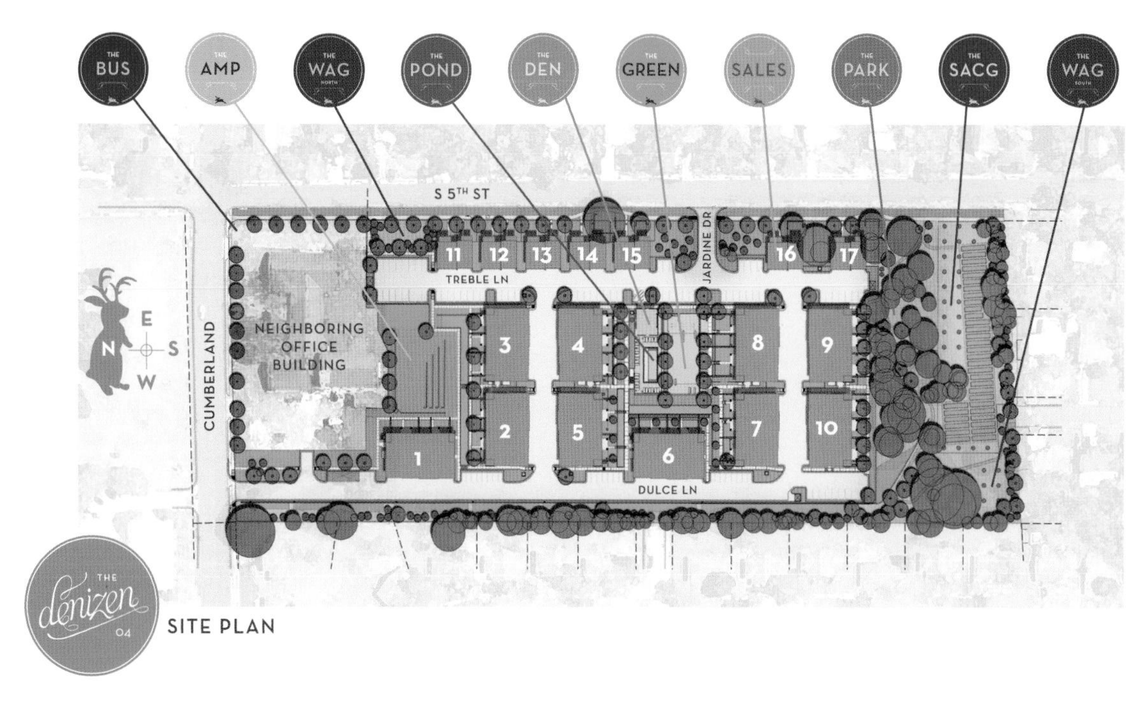

SITE PLAN

Austin is MG's home. The company works very hard to improve our home for all of our neighbors and friends.

Building the Future

Austin and its surrounding communities are in a period of explosive growth fueled by the confluence of good government, great education, incredible talent, artistic expression, entrepreneurial creativity, and capital resources. Every person in our community both needs and deserves

(continued on next page)

a quality environment in which to live and work.

MG Realty believes that the needs of Austin and its surrounding communities are best met by the creation of unique, live-work-play environments providing residents and employees walkable access to features and amenities that change their lives for the better. That goal pushes them to create unique places based on the specific needs of that neighborhood.

This relentless pursuit of serving others is reflected in the redevelopment (with able partners) of the RBJ Retirement Center land along Lady Bird Lake, which is an office/retail/residential community wrapped around a core of affordable housing for seniors capable of independent living.

MG will soon start construction of a new town center in Kyle, Texas. The development will feature housing, office, and retail, and is destined to become the city center for what has become one of the fastest-growing cities in the United States.

MG is also designing and building the town center portion of the Goodnight Ranch, a 6,500-home community, with a trail network, schools, pools, fitness facilities, community gathering places, and wellness areas that will make this community unique in South Austin.

Through Groundwork, MG is managing the design, approval, and creation of a 2,100-acre, mixed-use community destined to be home to almost 30,000 people with 12,000 jobs on-site. With three miles of Colorado River frontage, this community, presently called Austin Green, will convert an old sand and gravel excavation site into parkland and a livable community to benefit all of Austin.

Momark is proud to have had a hand in the design and creation of the Austonian, a 56-story luxury residential tower in the middle of Austin. Our recent Tyndall condominium community stands complete on the edge of downtown, providing housing for a diverse group of downtown citizens in a thriving, walkable environment. Momark also designs and builds affordable and attainable housing in unique locations, serving a broad cross-section of our citizenry.

People and Commitment to Service

The Company belives that nothing worthwhile happens without quality people. We do big things with a small staff of dedicated professionals who manage the complexity of our projects.

The partnership team of Terry Mitchell and Bob Gass bring over 65 years of development experience to our company. The company's Project Principals—Megan Shannon, Steven Spears, and Lydia Clay—each have earned a high degree of respect and trust in the network of sophisticated investors, government officials, architects, designers, engineers, planners, and attorneys who come together to make a unique project possible. They are the best in the business.

And yet, beyond all of the complexity of the work that MG Realty does for many stake-holders, there is one simple goal that governs everything they do. That goal is to serve Austin, both the Austin of today, and the city we will become in the future.

A Commitment to Doing More

IBC Bank traces its roots back to 1966 in Laredo, Texas where it all started with a group of investors working to meet the needs of small businesses. The IBC Bank system has proudly served the Austin Area for the past 15 years with the same community – minded service they started with 53 years ago.

IBC Bank's slogan "We Do More" reflects the bank's determined dedication to the growth and success of the customers and the communities it serves. The cornerstone on which the bank was founded remains a key focus of the bank's team members today - superior products and services tailored to the specific needs of its customers. IBC Bank's "Prompt Response" philosophy means traveling to a customer's place of business or working far beyond the mythical banker's hours. It also includes providing the right connections statewide and internationally, offering the bank's customers the resources and relationships that IBC Bank has spent decades developing. Most importantly, it is a reflection of IBC Bank's commitment to each of its customers.

In the summer of 2004, IBC Bank-Austin President & CEO Bob Barnes led IBC Bank's official full-banking service into the Austin market, which was marked by the opening of the bank's regional headquarters in downtown Austin. (In 2001, IBC Bank acquired Austin-based First Equity and made its initial footprint in the Austin market.) Barnes continues to spearhead IBC Bank-Austin's expansion in the greater Austin area organically through new branch construction and community reinvestment. IBC Bank-Austin currently has eleven branches in the greater Austin area including locations in Leander, Cedar Park, Round Rock, Bastrop, and a main location in East Austin at East Cesar Chavez St. and North Pleasant Valley Road that accommodates the underserved in that part of the city.

IBC is proud to have financed many local projects, including The Quincy, Hotel Magdalena, Music Lane, Plaza Saltillo, The Grove, State House Apartments, and Springtown Student Housing in San Marcos. Master Planned Communities include Belterra, Blackhawk, Caliterra, Carmel, Carneros Ranch, Crosswinds, Cypress Forest, Highpoint, Larkspur Community, North Paloma Lake, Parten Ranch Subdivision, Rough Hollow, Santa Rita Ranch, and Siena.

Full-Service Banking

Since its founding more than a half-century ago, IBC Bank has remained committed to streamlining the banking experience with its financial products and services. Customers can opt for IBC Bank's Free Checking Account with no minimum balance requirements and no monthly service charges or choose another checking or savings product that suits their needs. The bank offers a full range of banking services including checking accounts, savings accounts, certificates of deposit, mortgage loans, personal loans, commercial loans, wire transfers, and more.

Most recently, IBC Bank was pleased to announce its engagement with J.D. Power, a global leader in consumer insights, data, analytics, and advisory services that helps brands enhance and understand customer experience.

In 2018, J.D. Power began to measure IBC Bank's customer satisfaction with the service quality provided across the bank's branch network. Through this engagement, IBC Bank continues to apply its "We Do More" motto by more accurately measuring the quality of service the bank provides. The goal is to enhance IBC Bank's service skills and provide a great customer experience.

A Community Bank Serving the Community

The IBC Bank management team is fully committed to serving its customers and improving the quality of life in the communities it serves. IBC Bank set out to help its schools and communities with a program that not only assists schools in addressing attendance issues, but also provides students with real-life skills.

The Minitropolis® program concept was created by IBC Bank in 1996 as a tool to help teachers impart the importance and significance of financial literacy at a young age.

Minitropolis® mirrors a fully functioning mini-city that replicates a real-life community for students in elementary schools. The program offers an exciting, hands-on learning tool that allows teachers to apply classroom-learned concepts to real-life scenarios such as purchasing groceries and going to the post office. The goal is for students to master the basics of financial literacy, understand the importance of saving money as well as learn leadership skills that will help them as adults.

The Minitropolis® program has grown significantly since its inception. It is now in approximately 30 elementary schools throughout Texas, including Austin's Blackshear Elementary School, founded in 2015.

In addition, IBC Bank-Austin has Community Suites at the IBC Bank Plaza and Cesar Chavez locations. These spaces are donated year-round to local non-profits for business and event use free of charge. In 2018, the bank hosted over 35 organizations with a valued in-kind donation cost of over $66,000.

IBC Bank-Austin has also been a major sponsor for many events including American YouthWorks Help Clifford Help Kids, The Greater Austin Hispanic Chamber of Commerce Capital of Texas Awards, the Junior League of Austin Christmas Affair, the Make-A-Wish Foundation Over The Edge event, the Muscular Dystrophy Association Muscle Walk, Blue Lapis Light performances, and Preservation Austin Merit Awards Celebration. The bank also strongly supports many other organizations that benefit low/moderate income individuals and organizations that impact the improvement of the Greater Austin Area. In addition, IBC Bank-Austin is a major supporter of the Seton Foundation in support of the Dell Seton Medical Center at The University of Texas in their mission to care for all by providing healthcare to families in our community who are living in poverty and otherwise could not afford care.

In recognition of its exemplary service to the community, IBC Bank-Austin has garnered numerous industry awards, most recently being named the 2018 Corporation of the Year by the Greater Austin Hispanic Chamber of Commerce at the 45th Celebrando Austin Gala. This award honors corporations that strongly support the chamber and proactively use their resources to give back to the Greater Austin community.

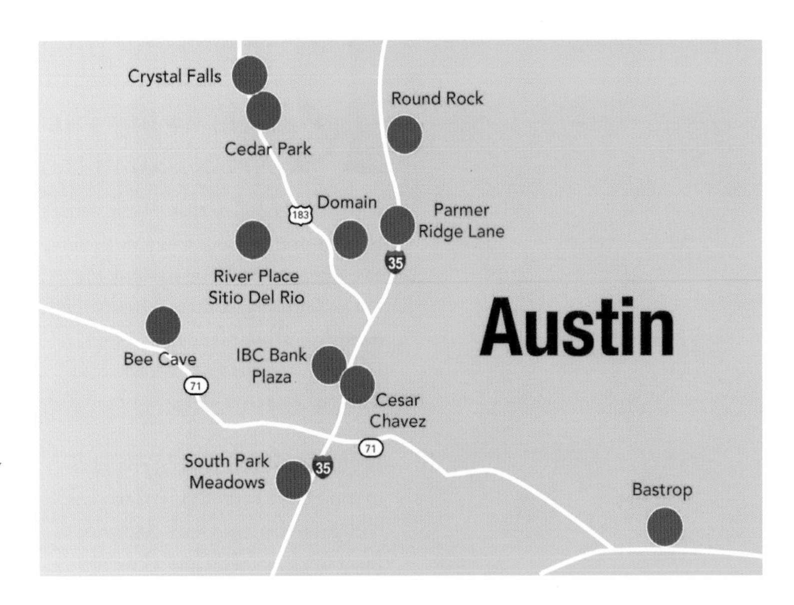

◄◄▲ Opposite page, above—Blue Lapis Light aerial performance on IBC Bank Plaza building – Fall 2014
Photo by Early McGehee

◄◄ Opposite page—IBC Bank Plaza – 500 W. 5th Street, Austin, TX
Photo by Jim Innes

▼ Incoming/Outgoing City Council Reception at IBC Bank Plaza Community Suite 2/6/15
Photo by Jim Innes

Access to Culture

A Focus on Diversity, Business Etiquette, and International Protocol

RESEARCH HAS SHOWN THAT THE SUCCESS OF BUSINESS PROFESSIONALS IN TODAY'S GLOBAL MARKETPLACE DEPENDS ON INTERACTION WITH THEIR COUNTERPARTS WORLDWIDE WHETHER IN THE BOARDROOM, OVER A MEAL, OR IN A VIRTUAL SETTING. SAVVY PROFESSIONALS KNOW THERE IS AN APPROPRIATE WAY TO INTERACT with colleagues. For that reason, many of those professionals today are turning to experts to help them navigate the often-confusing world of introductions, handshakes, body language, dining etiquette, and the myriad nuances of cultures across our globe.

In 2006, Sharon Schweitzer decided to combine her travel experience, legal background, people skills, and passion for entrepreneurship into a business entity that would assist in that navigation. She launched Access to Culture to cultivate an awareness of domestic and global cultural differences while fostering an appreciation of diversity, business etiquette, and international protocol.

Access to Culture serves today as a cross-cultural business consulting company that assists highly motivated individuals, teams, and organizations with finding solutions to their cultural business challenges and strengthening global business relationships. The underlying goal is to facilitate leadership development in the borderless workplace by focusing on competencies needed to bridge cultural differences. To begin the process, Access to Culture uses comprehensive, statistically valid self-assessments based on empirical research, including the IDI, GCI, or IES which measure a wide range of competencies. The feedback is discussed and a development plan is created to leverage strengths and address any gaps.

"We strive to cultivate an understanding of domestic and global cultural differences while fostering an appreciation of diversity," Sharon explains. "We commit our energy to extending hospitality to international visitors, encouraging citizen ambassadors, and sharing knowledge. We provide the tools for leaders to develop global acumen, problem-solving skills, adaptable thinking, cultural competency, and intelligence.

"Access to Culture is rooted in values that foster trust, inspire respect, enhance understanding, and shape empathetic leaders and organizations to build bridges across cultures. Our key values are to commit to integrity, reduce conflict, encourage diversity, and share resources."

Building Relationships

Sharon's team focuses on creating customized programs individually tailored to each client. Assistance is offered in numerous fields such as:

- High profile and VIP guest preparation
- Extending the invitation
- Protocol officer duties
- Receiving lines
- Country-specific briefings
- Business etiquette
- Bridging cultures with international customers, and others

"Our customized service for our clients sets us apart from our competition," Sharon states. "We conduct a client strength and needs assessment before beginning any project. We don't use a 'cookie cutter' approach. We provide Executive Summaries of participant evaluations so a ROI can be calculated. We conduct an annual client satisfaction survey to determine how we can continuously improve."

Realizing that relationship building is an integral part of business success, Access to Culture training is designed to build confidence, poise, and finesse to business networking encounters by focusing on the do's and taboos of professional encounters, including:

- Appropriate conversational topics
- Body language
- Acting as an ambassador
- Toasting and responding

- Global tipping
- Buffet and beverage etiquette, and numerous others

"Food is part of culture," Sharon points out. "Worldwide, many business deals are sealed with meals, so it is important to know the difference between eating and dining."

Success on a Global Stage

Clients from across the globe, from Chile to the Czech Republic, have availed themselves of Access to Culture's services. Many of the most recognizable names across a broad spectrum of professional fields, including business, telecommunications, medicine, and others have turned to Access to Culture to provide practical techniques for improving business communication and increasing revenue.

J.P. Morgan Chase, USA is numbered among Sharon's many satisfied clients. "Sharon's knowledge of culture, her in-depth multicultural experiences, and her examples provided our teams with more than we anticipated. We dramatically increased the odds of win-win when negotiating."

Officials at MD Anderson were equally impressed. "Sharon Schweitzer was the perfect instructor and etiquette expert. Sharon's presentations at MD Anderson for our professional development were exceptional. Her warm personality, enthusiasm, and passion made the sessions an educational pleasure for our MD Anderson audience. Our professional staff provided overwhelmingly positive feedback, her substantive materials were impressive, and I very much enjoyed working with Sharon."

Sharon has appeared on CBS, NBC, ABC, FOX, and BBC News, and speaks at ALA, Big Ten Academic Alliance, and SXSW conferences as an expert in cross-cultural business. In addition, she is the author of the Amazon Number One best-selling book in International Business, Access to Asia, named to Kirkus Reviews' Best Books of 2015 and now in its third printing. Sharon's expertise in Asia led to her serving as the Chinese Ceremonial Dining Etiquette Specialist for the documentary series "Confucius Was a Foodie" on NatGeo's People.

Her Access to Culture blog was named one of the "Top 10 Intercultural Communication Blogs" in 2017, a year after she received the prestigious recognition of being named the winner of the British Airways "International Trade, Investment & Expansion Award" (small business category) at the Greater Austin Business Awards.

Whether helping professionals achieve confidence in conducting global business, preparing university students for international careers, or assisting meeting planners in selecting the perfect wines for a dinner, Access to Culture is recognized as the go-to source for professional training and assistance.

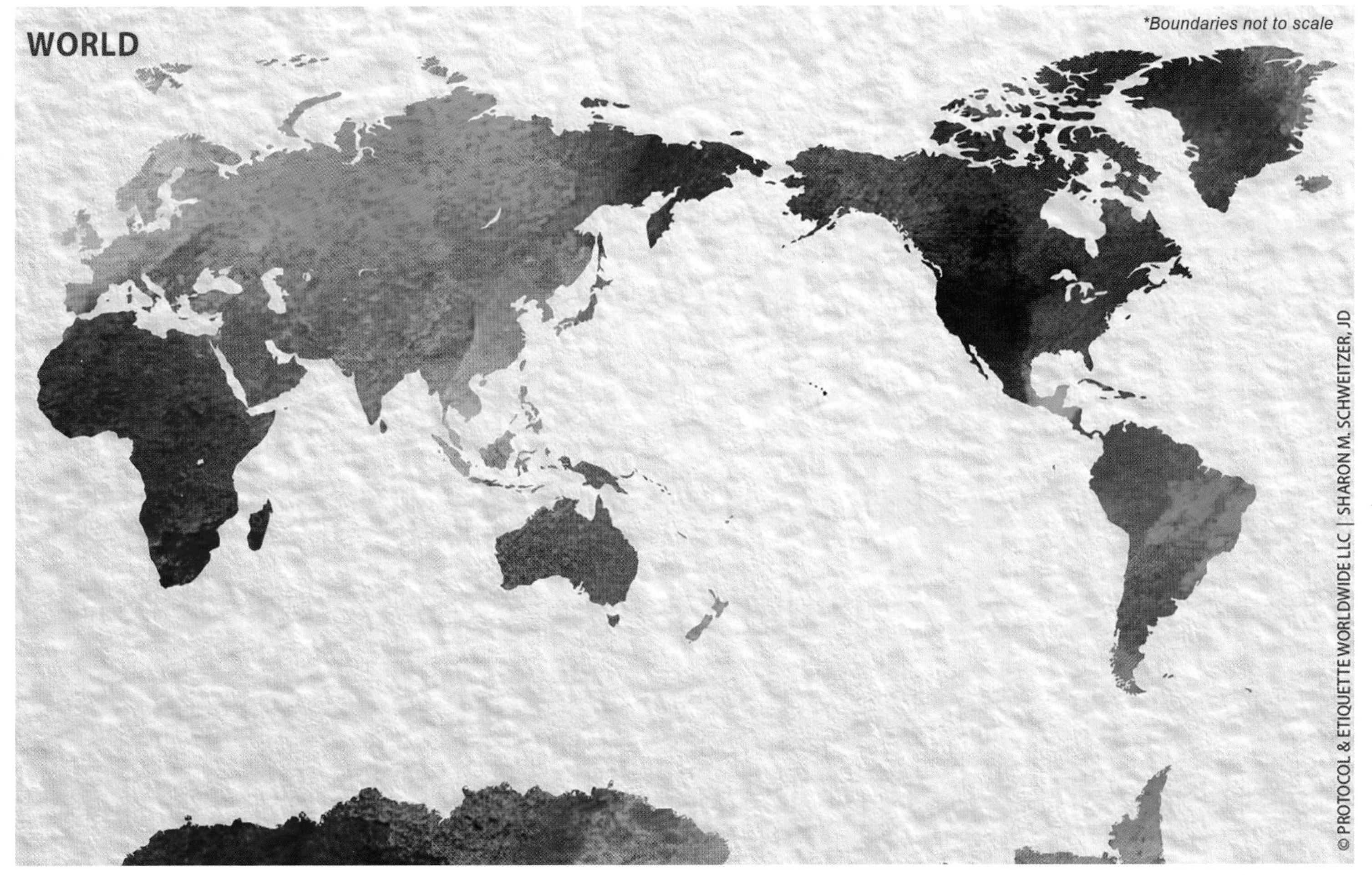

Creating Transformational Projects

Austin native Matt Whelan founded RedLeaf Properties in 2009 as a real estate developer focusing on projects that would deliver significant community benefit. Rob Shands and Bryan Kaminski joined the firm soon after and continued its goal of blending a creative, entrepreneurial approach with corporate discipline.

A decade after its founding, the RedLeaf team continues to excel at working in partnership with public entities to create large-scale, mixed-use projects that include vibrant commercial districts and inviting residential neighborhoods. The firm's projects are known for creating remarkable experiences, setting new standards for sustainability, and delivering tangible and intangible value for the full range of project stakeholders.

"We understand the intricacies of public-private partnerships," Whelan states. "We have robust experience navigating the fast-paced private real estate markets as well as the demanding requirements and transparency required by public agencies. Our entrepreneurial mindset gives us the flexibility to address the unique needs of both the private and public sectors, while our disciplined development approach enables us to navigate demanding planning and reporting requirements.

"Where others see challenges, we see possibility. We pursue development opportunities where we can unlock value and deliver long-term community benefits using creative, locally tailored approaches. We understand the value of meaningful experiences and personal connections and recognize their potential to energize individuals and encourage engagement. With this in mind, we create sustainable, inclusive places that support healthy lifestyles and strengthen communities."

A Distinctive Signature

RedLeaf's principals have acquired a unique depth of experience by executing projects totaling more than five million square feet and covering over 3,300 acres. Together, their experience includes a wide spectrum of property types which are home to thousands of residents, thriving retail, corporate headquarters, government buildings, hospitals, colleges and universities.

Among the firm's most notable projects is the redevelopment of Highland Mall. The project is the adaptive re-use and redevelopment of Austin's first enclosed regional mall. RedLeaf led the effort to form a public-private partnership with Austin Community College to acquire and redevelop this important community asset. The award-winning project's development team worked closely with stakeholders and community leaders to create a project that benefits residents throughout the region, supports surrounding neighborhoods, protects the environment, and honors the site's history.

RedLeaf's efforts led to an "Overall Winner" award from the Austin Business Journal and an "Innovation Award" from the Urban Land Institute.

"RedLeaf Properties is a visionary firm that treats developments as more than just projects," noted Dr. Richard Rhodes, the President and CEO of Austin Community College. "They seek to create properties that are sustainable and well-loved by the community."

▲ Park opening under relocated Heritage Tree

▲ Fontaine Plaza Park

▼ Highland Mall redevelopment

Circuit of The Americas (COTA)

A Playground for Today with Memories Forever

Circuit of The Americas (COTA) is a 1,500-acre world-class sports and entertainment complex located in Southeast Austin. The facility is truly a multi-purpose venue for racing, music, sports, big events, and fun.

COTA contains:

- The nation's only "grade 1" circuit and host to the Formula 1 United States Grand Prix, MotoGP, the IndyCar Classic, the FIM Road Racing World Championship, Historic Car races, and The National University Solar Car Challenge.
- Austin360 Amphitheater, the largest outdoor stage in Texas, with a capacity of 14,000 people. Designed by award-winning architect, Juan Miro, the Austin360 Amphitheater is spectacularly designed for acoustic excellence. The theater was named *USA TODAY*'s "10 Best Concert Venues Across the USA" and Pollstar's "2013 Best New Venue"
- Superstage Concert Lawn with a capacity of 83,000 people
- 25-story Landmark Observation Tower - recipient of the prestigious American Institute of Architecture 2013 Award, along with many other awards.
- 44,000-square foot event center, including the COTA café.
- 270,000-square foot Pit/Paddock Building with 34 garage bays and two upper levels of hospitality suites, accommodating 5,000 people
- One-mile high-speed, public karting track
- 6,000-seat USL Championship soccer and multi-purpose stadium
- 12-story starting grid view zip line ride
- Premium ReV Line RV park with 78 spaces and year-round operations
- On-site parking for 25,000 vehicles

Inspiration and Dedication

What evolved into F-1's "Best Race of the Year" in 2018 and Motorsport World Expo's "Motorsport Facility of the Year" was originally planned to be a housing development. After numerous delays, the project eventually ran into the housing market bust and sat idle. The primary investor, Bobby Epstein, told friends at the time that he often envisioned an amusement area inspired by Arlington, Texas. Epstein believed Central Texas would be a perfect place to create a similar sports and entertainment destination zone. In 2009, Epstein was introduced to fellow Texan Tavo Hellmund, a racing enthusiast who was looking for someone to embrace his vision to bring Formula One to Austin. After more than a year of planning, the two men approached Texas billionaire Red McCombs to join them in their pursuit. McCombs, a successful automotive businessman, former owner of the Minnesota Vikings, two NBA teams, and founder of Clear Channel Communications, agreed to be the "lead" investor and gave the project instant power.

In an effort to complete construction in a short window and fighting numerous weather delays, 1,200 hard-working, talented craftsmen and laborers kept a twenty-hour daily work site moving. The Circuit opened with the Formula One United States Grand Prix on November 18, 2012.

It did not take long for the accolades to begin pouring in. Just a year after hosting its first race, the *Sports Business Journal* awarded COTA the 2012 USGP "Event of the Year." After its opening in 2013, the Austin360 Amphitheater received *Pollstar*'s "Global Best New Venue" award.

An Economic Powerhouse

COTA attracts visitors from across the country and around the world. The financial gains for Texas and the local area have been staggering, with COTA generating in excess of five billion dollars of economic impact. With 150 full-time employees and a part-time, event-based workforce, along with being the largest taxpayer in the southeastern portion of the county, COTA's local impact is making a real difference. The facility puts a special emphasis on hiring local students and neighborhood residents, fills hotel rooms and restaurants region-wide, and attracts tourists for local businesses. COTA events generate in excess of $10 million of direct and indirect tips/gratuities, and the beneficiaries of those dollars are often people for whom the income is meaningfully necessary.

A Community Partner

With a focus on veterans and military families, "at risk" youth, and medical research focused on diseases affecting the elderly, COTA helps local non-profits raise money for worthy causes through the donation of race and concert tickets, on-track experiences, venue space, and official memorabilia. Finally, to demonstrate a strong commitment to community giving, full-time employees receive three full paid days per year to do volunteer work.

Circuit of The Americas is proud to be part of the Greater Austin community, and the COTA team is committed to giving back to its neighbors and the wonderful people, places, and organizations that make Central Texas a great place to live, work, and play.

Partnering With Austin

WHILE RUDY GARZA CONTINUES TO SERVE AS PRESIDENT AND CEO OF THE COMPANY HE FOUNDED IN AUSTIN IN 2012, HE CREDITS HIS FAMILY FOR BEING HIS INSPIRATION AND SUPPORT. "ALTHOUGH MY FATHER NEVER MADE IT BIG OR HAD A VERY ELABORATE BUSINESS MODEL, HE WENT FROM BEING a migrant worker to owning his own roofing company until the day he died," Rudy explained.

▲ Rudy and Melissa Garza.
▶▲ Rudy's parents, Raul and Asteria Garza. Although both have passed, they continue to inspire Rudy today.

▼▶ Garza Team members giving back.
▼ Josh Villarreal supporting the annual Salvation Army Rock the Red Kettle. Garza Team Members giving back.

"I have always been inspired by what he was able to accomplish. I know he struggled and had difficult times, but through all his efforts and dedication, he made it work and he was very good at it." Garza also credits his wife, Melissa, with being his "coach, confidant, and biggest partner in establishing and growing the firm."

That growth has been impressive. Garza EMC is a civil engineering firm providing design consulting for land development as well as design of public works infrastructure. Headquartered in Austin with two offices in the capital city, the firm covers all the major markets in Texas with offices in Houston and San Antonio.

Since its inception, Garza's focus has been to establish genuine, authentic relationships with each and every client that looks to them for the highest quality professional services. The underlying goal is to make sure that those clients understand that Garza professionals are truly their partner in their project and not just a professional convenience.

▼ Team Garza rebuilding the boardwalk for the Austin Nature and Science Center.

◀ Team Garza at the Water for People Volleyball Tournament.

Those professionals work to get to know their clients, their goals, objectives, what works for them and what doesn't, and earn their trust. The Garza team members are recognized experts in the industry. They work hard to ensure that they are providing not only the highest quality technical services, but remaining focused on their commitment to ensuring the successful completion of each project entrusted to them by their clients.

That focus and their client-oriented approach has led to Garza's growth and success.

A Trusted Partner

Following a 23-year career in the public sector, with the last 20 of those years in city government, Rudy Garza felt he was prepared for the next chapter in his professional life. Garza served as Assistant City Manager for the City of Austin and had a first-hand opportunity to witness the true entrepreneurial spirit of the city. "Local businesses are sincerely recognized as a true benefit and value in Austin," Rudy stated, "and I felt there was no better place to get started."

As a business owner, Garza quickly recognized his number one asset. "It is undoubtedly our team members," he states. "In order to deliver a successful project to our clients, we must begin with taking care of our employees. Our focus has been, and remains today, ensuring our employees have an environment where they feel safe, comfortable, respected, have the ability to grow and develop, and have FUN! Our corporate culture is one where we truly support the entire person and recognize and understand that there is so much to every person. They can offer their life experiences to help us all be better at what we do. I feel privileged to have a great group of associates onboard, and I am grateful every day to be surrounded by some really awesome people."

Those team members have completed some of Austin's most impressive landmarks:

- Dell Seton Hospital
- Austin State Hospital
- Schwab corporate campus
- New Travis County Courthouse
- Austin FC Major League Soccer Stadium
- University of Texas Medical School
- Two corporate campuses for a major international technology company
- State of Texas Capital Complex
- Austin Energy Headquarters
- Multiple K12 schools serving the community

Giving Something Back

Rudy and his team lead by example in their commitment to give something back to the community that has been their home. "We are truly grateful and appreciative for all the opportunities we have been provided to be successful, and we feel we have an obligation to give back to the community," Rudy points out. "This obligation guides us to help various charitable organizations, but also to stay involved in the issues and matters that are impacting our community, such as school bonds, transportation plans, economic development policies, employment policies, and many others.

"Our team is involved in many local organizations, including the Greater Austin Chamber of Commerce, Real Estate Council of Austin, Leadership Austin, and the Salvation Army. While we support many great charitable organizations in the area, we have decided that we can make the biggest impact by focusing the majority of our financial and people resources to the Salvation Army.

"Working on major projects in the area has given us the opportunity to impact our community, and I consider those opportunities as a gift."

"For where your treasure is, there your heart will be." Matthew 6:21
▼ Rudy's treasure is absolutely his family. His daily motivation, all the joy in his life, comes from his family. Pictured here are Rudy and Melissa's daughters, grandchildren, and sons-in-law's, enjoying life and being silly.

A Century Strong & Still Growing

Baylor Scott & White Health (BSWH) ranks as the largest not-for-profit healthcare system in Texas and one of the largest in the United States. The organization's birth was in 2013 with the combination of North Texas-based Baylor Health Care System and Temple-based Scott & White Healthcare. Its roots, however, date back to 1897.

It was then that each healthcare system began its century of providing hope, healing, and medical breakthroughs to millions of Texans, including those living in the Austin area. For more than 11 years, residents in the northern part of the Austin metropolitan area have become part of the system's growing history. Shortly after combining, BSWH began focusing on bringing its legacy of healing and mission of promoting the overall wellbeing of individuals, families, and communities in the Austin area by establishing the company's Baylor Scott & White - Austin/Round Rock Region.

The organization has maintained an intense focus on expansion into and around Austin that has become essential to BSWH's strategy and long-term success:

- Austin is among the fastest growing markets in the nation.
- BSWH is focused on increasing Texans' access to quality, affordable healthcare.
- Austin is a major hub for technology and innovation, allowing Baylor Scott & White to pilot innovative care models that can be advanced throughout the integrated delivery network.

Currently, the BSWH Austin/Round Rock Region consists of eight hospitals and more than 70 locations throughout the Greater Austin area. The primary service areas include the five-county region of Travis, Williamson, Hays, Caldwell, and Bastrop. Additionally, patients from Texas Hill Country counties are served by BSWH facilities in the Greater Austin area, as well as the organization's medical centers and clinics in and around Marble Falls and Llano.

An Integrated Approach to Care Close to Home

Giving communities and patients access to the innovative care and services BSWH offers is essential to furthering its not-for-profit mission and bettering the overall health of Texans. This novel, seamless approach is different from many of its peers in the Austin

area and beyond in that it features a highly skilled team that provides integrated care not only within a single clinic or hospital, but between all BSWH facilities in Central Texas, as they are all connected through a single electronic health record. In addition, BSWH focuses not only on medical treatment, but also on overall care and wellness through programs offering healthy cooking classes, leading regular walks on local park trails, and other initiatives.

Convenient access to healthcare is key. BSWH facilities are strategically located to make access to care in the congested Austin area easier, with many locations offering same-day appointments along with weekend and after-hours care.

The large number of medical specialties and subspecialties that BSWH offers has made it a major participant in research and clinical trials, with the ability to connect patients in need of some of the latest therapies being studied for a wide range of conditions.

"We are focused on providing integrated healthcare to patients closer to where they live and work, using advanced technologies and featuring a team focused on creating an exceptional care experience," says Jay Fox, BSWH Austin/Round Rock Region president.

Improving the Healthcare Landscape

Central to BSWH Austin/Round Rock Region's efforts to make healthcare better is innovation applied in numerous ways. The BSWH downtown Austin clinic is referred to as the organization's "innovation hub" featuring fresh technologies – such as iPads for patient check-in and touch screens in patient rooms – which allow for interactive patient visits. In addition, the use of robots enables critical care specialists to remotely evaluate patients at BSWH intensive care units in smaller communities. The BSWH smartphone app has become the highest rated patient care application in the Apple store. The app allows patients to enjoy a new level of convenience for scheduling appointments, refilling prescriptions, reviewing results, messaging care providers, and initiating eVisits or video visits without a trip to the doctor's office.

These and other cutting-edge innovations have led to numerous nationally recognized awards and certifications, including a listing of Baylor Scott & White Medical Center – Round Rock as among the nation's Top 100 Hospitals by a national healthcare rating agency.

In addition to bettering the overall health of patients in the region, BSWH has had an economic impact across the greater Austin area. The system has become an important employer with more than 400 physicians and advanced practice professionals supported by a team of more than 2,600 clinical and support staff. "We're also helping shape the economy of the area by not only employing thousands of people, but by helping keep the Austin workforce healthy," Fox added.

The BSWH Austin/Round Rock Region also is extremely active in supporting community health, wellness, and other impactful community improvement in initiatives. In 2018 alone, the Austin/Round Rock Region hosted, facilitated, or otherwise provided key support for 31 programs and 379 events benefitting the community that were held at local BSWH facilities, area schools, businesses, community centers, and other locations.

Meanwhile, BSWH employees of the region provided more than 3,700 hours of community benefit-related service in 2018.

Setting the Standard for Prosthetics and Orthotics

FROM THE DREAM OF AN ORTHOPEDIC ENGINEER IN EARLY TWENTIETH-CENTURY GERMANY TO THE GLOBAL LEADER IN PROSTHETICS A CENTURY LATER, THE STORY OF OTTOBOCK HAS BEEN A JOURNEY FOCUSING ON HELPING MORE PEOPLE RESTORE OR RETAIN THEIR MOBILITY. OTTO BOCK, AN ORTHOPEDIC ENGINEER LIVING IN BERLIN IN 1919, ENVISIONED MASS-PRODUCED PROSTHETIC COMPONENTS TO IMPROVE THE FITTING FOR TENS OF thousands of veterans returning from World War I. The "Henry Ford" of the prosthetics industry, Otto Bock founded Orthopädische Industrie GmbH in Berlin, but later moved to Königsee, Thuringia.

Otto Bock revolutionized prosthetics with his ideas, and soon expanded activities outside the German market. His son-in-law, Dr. Max Näder, helped to found the first foreign branch of the company, now known as Ottobock, in Minneapolis, Minnesota in 1958. In 1990, Bock's grandson, Professor Hans Georg Näder, assumed management of the company that has now become a global brand with locations in more than 55 countries.

To dramatically change the approach to doing business, Ottobock relocated its North American headquarters to Austin in 2014. The city's entrepreneurial and tech business environment offered a digitally driven approach to accelerating growth, as well as a developing local medical device community.

A FOCUS ON PEOPLE

Celebrating its centennial anniversary in 2019, Ottobock takes great pride in its adherence to its core values - human, reliable, inventive. The goal is to improve the quality of life of Ottobock's end-users enabling them to live independent daily lives.

Ottobock manufactures prosthetic and orthotic devices across all categories. In prosthetics, Ottobock launched C-Leg, the world's first fully microprocessor controlled knee in 1999. Every iteration of the C-Leg continually improves on the control strategies that enable real time adaptation to the wearer's gait, changes in surface or speed, even when traversing unstable ground, stairs, or ramps.

◀ The Ottobock C-Leg® microprocessor knee was launched in the United States in 1999, and is now in its fourth generation.

For orthotics, Ottobock's marque product is C-Brace – the world's first orthosis using microprocessor sensor technology, which controls both the stance and swing phase hydraulically. It supports the user during the entire gait cycle and adapts to everyday situations in real time.

"Ottobock has brought over 100 jobs to Austin and over $10 million in annual payroll and capital investments in the same magnitude," stated Brad Ruhl, Managing Director, North America. "But more than that we have established a presence in the welcoming community of Austin that creates awareness of our purpose to help people regain their freedom of movement.

"We are connected to the Dell Seton Medical Center at The University of Texas, The Army Futures Command, SXSW, YTexas and the offices of the Mayor of Austin and the Governor of Texas. We also give back to the community through Lifeworks, Keep Austin Beautiful, Austin Speechlab, Boys and Girls Club, and provide resources to the Andy Roddick Foundation in addition to our contributions on a national level. We have become a fine citizen of Austin, Texas and a caring neighbor."

▲ The Ottobock C-Brace® is the world's first mechatronic stance and swing phase control orthosis (SSCO®).

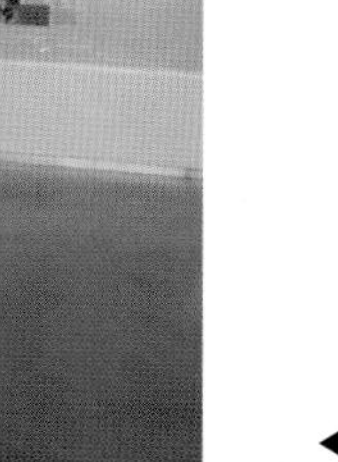

◀ Showroom at the Ottobock North America Headquarters in Austin, Texas

Powering Austin's Growth

Texas Gas Service is the third-largest natural gas distribution company in Texas. Located in Austin, they provide natural gas to more than 260,000 customers in the greater Austin area. Its parent company, ONE Gas Inc, is one of the largest publicly traded, 100 percent regulated natural gas utilities in the U.S.

The Texas Gas Service story began quite humbly in West Texas almost 100 years ago, when it was known as Southern Union Gas. Southern Union grew and acquired properties in Austin, El Paso, Galveston, the Rio Grande Valley, and other regions of Texas, now part of the Texas Gas Service territory. In 2003, Southern Union was renamed Texas Gas Service. The company has third generation employees and is proud to say their customers are also their families, friends, and neighbors.

The mission of Texas Gas Service is to deliver natural gas for a better tomorrow. Day in and day out, they work hard to serve their customers and communities, because a positive impact today empowers a better tomorrow.

Natural Gas is Vital

Natural gas is a crucial part of our daily lives and plays a critical role in the future of energy independence. Every day, customers rely on natural gas to warm homes, cook meals, dry laundry, and take hot showers. It is also relied upon for electricity. That's right, natural gas helps lessen the load on the Texas electrical grid, which is vital due to increasing power supply demand.

Natural Gas is Sustainable and Clean

Natural gas is a clean energy source and will continue to be an important part of renewable energy solutions, such as wind and solar. Energy-related U.S. carbon emissions are at 25-year lows due to increases in natural gas efficiency and renewable energy growth. Homes are using natural gas more efficiently, accounting for only four percent of total U.S. greenhouse gas emissions.

Natural gas is truly homemade energy – domestic reserves are producing at record highs with the U.S. now a net exporter of natural gas to Mexico and Canada. Moving toward energy independence, natural gas will help strengthen national security and increase jobs for Americans – including in Austin.

Benefits of Natural Gas

Think of your favorite restaurant or home-cooked meal. Chances are the chef used natural gas to prepare those meals. Natural gas is the preferred choice for many chefs who create masterpieces in the kitchen or on the grill. Natural gas has many benefits, some of which you can taste, some of

▲ Meals on Wheels and More grant

▲ Habitat for Humanity Home Build

which you can feel (in a warm home or hot shower) and some that show up in your pocketbook.

- Affordable – Homes that use natural gas for cooking, water and space heating along with clothes drying spend less money – on average – compared to homes using electricity for those same appliances.
- Reliable – Natural gas systems have demonstrated reliability, even during challenging weather conditions, such as hurricanes.
- Resilient – Use of natural gas to generate electricity has grown substantially in recent years as companies look to better manage peak energy needs. Added resiliency supports the growing trend that is expected to continue as the demand for more and cleaner energy arises.

Investing in the Community

Texas Gas Service employees volunteer with organizations such as United Way, Special Olympics, Habitat for Humanity, Helping Hands Homes and Ronald McDonald House. And, for more than 20 years, their employees have delivered meals for Meals on Wheels and More.

Austin employees serve on the boards of important civic and non-profit organizations, such as the Greater Austin Chamber of Commerce, Downtown Austin Alliance, Greater Hispanic Chamber, Network of Asian American Organizations, Leadership Austin and Caritas of Austin.

These efforts extend beyond volunteering and include financial contributions — both as a company and individually. The ONE Gas Foundation makes grants to non-profit organizations, most recently, to the Boys and Girls Clubs of Austin, St. Edward's University, The Trail Foundation, and the Austin Parks Foundation. The philanthropic arm also matches employee contributions.

Outreach Programs Within the Community

Established in 1993, their Energy Efficiency Program was one of the first natural gas programs in the country. The Program, in partnership with the City of Austin and Austin Energy, offers customers and homebuilders rebates for high-efficiency natural gas appliances and energy-saving home improvement measures. In 2018, Texas Gas Service issued more than $2.28 million in incentives to qualifying customers.

Annually, the company provides almost $400,000 of free natural gas equipment to low-income and elderly customers in need. They also partner with community agencies to provide energy assistance to senior citizens, individuals with disabilities, and those whose immediate financial resources simply cannot cover home-heating expenses through Share the Warmth.

Additionally, they support public school foundations across Texas to fund grants that help teachers equip classrooms with the latest technology and create programs to prepare students for the future, including the Austin Ed Fund, which supports the Austin Independent School District.

Safety is Key

Safety is the top priority of Texas Gas Service. They continuously improve the safety of their system and work to educate customers through multimedia channels, live events, and media outreach. Keeping gas in the pipe reduces the number of incidents and helps to keep customers, communities, and employees safe and warm.

Texas Gas Service is proud to serve Austin and looks forward to a better tomorrow for everyone.

▼ Austin Heart Walk employee event

An Advocate for Business in the Austin Region

SINCE 1878 THE GREATER AUSTIN CHAMBER OF COMMERCE HAS TAKEN ON THE BIGGEST CHALLENGES FACING BUSINESSES IN AUSTIN, FROM ADVOCATING FOR A POLICY ENVIRONMENT THAT ENCOURAGES GROWTH TO INVESTING IN GROWING THE REGIONAL TALENT PIPELINE AND CONNECTING BUSINESSES THROUGH membership and events. The Chamber's award-winning team is a key factor in why the Austin region has experienced incredible job growth. From 2004 to 2018, the Austin region has generated more net new jobs on a percentage basis than any other top 50 major metro in the U.S.

▲ The delegation of business and community leaders closing out the annual DC advocacy trip.

The Chamber helps bring job creators to the region and serves as a pivotal partner in helping local companies expand their businesses. It is a membership organization that helps create jobs so people can secure work, provide for their families, and achieve prosperity.

The Chamber team understands that Austin is a one-of-a-kind place that defies stereotypes. The city is progressive and fiercely entrepreneurial; pro-business and pro-environment; easy going and hardworking. The Austin region won't just welcome businesses; it will make them better.

SETTING PRIORITIES

Keenly aware of the competition among cities for hosting business events, professional meetings, and attracting businesses to their metro areas, the professional staff at the Austin Chamber has identified key areas in which they work hard to showcase the city's business climate. They play a key role in shaping a policy environment that helps fuel the local economy, addresses affordability, and helps people succeed. The Chamber diligently works with policymakers and elected officials to make this a reality.

▼ A group of delegates attended the 2019 InterCity Visit to the Twin Cities.

The Chamber team is a key factor in why the Austin region has experienced phenomenal job growth and prosperity since 2004. Numerous Chamber-sponsored programs have been instrumental in helping bring job creators to the region and are pivotal partners in helping local companies expand their businesses.

The Chamber's economic development specialists provide expertise to potential businesses in discovering the Austin community and identifying and analyzing the perfect spot for a business looking to relocate to the area. Staff members with experience in this field provide assistance in the site selection process across the diverse communities that make up the Austin region. They help identify the location of choice against other major markets for the retention, expansion, and attraction of jobs and investment.

In addition, the Chamber team focuses on the established businesses that are already headquartered in Austin and providing jobs across the region. The Chamber's Connect First program is one of several initiatives which strengthen the organization's relationship with its members by supporting the success and growth of these companies. The Chamber serves as a one-stop center for confidential support in a company's site selection project, including real estate, research, and facilitation of all aspects of the process through to final negotiations with the selected community.

AN INTERNATIONAL STAGE

The Austin Chamber does not limit its activities to attracting potential businesses from across the United States. The Austin Global Gateway (AGG) is a Greater Austin Chamber program. AGG acknowledges that while Austin has already established its status for domestic U.S. corporations, the city's reputation among foreign business leaders has lagged. The AGG executive committee endeavors to correct this disparity by leveraging its member relationships to demonstrate Austin's comparative advantage to discriminating investors, creative entrepreneurs, and dynamic corporations worldwide.

The Chamber team actively advocates for the innovation community by providing thought leadership and strategy. They focus on attracting and retaining talent, increasing capital, growing and diversifying the innovation ecosystem, and leveraging local universities for increased commercialization.

The Chamber's commitment to the future is evident in programs designed to cultivate future generations of entrepreneurs. The Austin Chamber and Austin ISD founded Austin Partners in

Education (APIE) in 1983. The primary function of APIE is to recruit, train, and place volunteers in the classroom once a week, every week of the school year. Once screened and trained by APIE, volunteers provide academic support to students in a small interactive group learning model via Classroom Coaching programs. In 2019, more than 850 Classroom Coaches joined an additional 800 mentors as APIE volunteers in Austin ISD. The Chamber's investment in local high school students helps prepare them for success in college, careers, or the military.

Opportunity Austin, a prosperity initiative serving five counties and launched by the Chamber in 2004, has helped create 423,600 jobs. That has resulted in Austin becoming the fastest-growing job market by percentage; contributed to a 63 percent increase in jobs in the region; helped the region achieve one of the lowest unemployment rates in the country; and much more.

A Track Record of Success

The work of the Chamber has been recognized with numerous awards, the most recent of which was the 2019 Mac Conway Award given annually to the top economic development organization in the U.S.

"As advocates for the business community, everything we do is for our members and their employees," stated Mike Rollins, the Chamber's President and CEO. "When the business community thrives, so do Austinites. We are proud of the jobs we've helped create in our region. As we help bring more jobs to the region that increase regional payroll, we increase the number of opportunities for people to achieve prosperity. On top of our thriving economy, we offer an unmatched quality of life."

▲ Kristin Marcum, President of Elizabeth Christian Public Relations, speaks at the annual Austin Gives Generous Business Awards event.

◀ Greater Austin Business Executive Leadership Award winners Tamara Fields with Accenture and Karen Box with Southwest Minority Supplier Development Council

▼ CeCe's Veggie Co. celebrates winning the 2019 A-List Awards.

Representing Austin's Hispanic Entrepreneurs

IN 2015 THE GREATER AUSTIN HISPANIC CHAMBER OF COMMERCE (GAHCC) WAS NAMED HISPANIC CHAMBER OF THE YEAR BY THE U.S. HISPANIC CHAMBER OF COMMERCE AT ITS ANNUAL MEETING IN HOUSTON, THE LARGEST GATHERING OF HISPANIC BUSINESS LEADERS IN THE COUNTRY. MORE RECENTLY, the GAHCC's Hispanic Austin Leadership Program was named one

of the top seven Hispanic Chamber Leadership programs in the country for its outstanding seventeen years of community impact. This honor comes from Lideramos, the National Alliance of Latino Leadership Programs.

These honors and other peer awards garnered by the GAHCC are indicative of the impact the organization has had on the Austin region since its inception in 1973. The Chamber was launched by 25 prominent Austin Hispanic leaders including former Mayor Gustavo "Gus" Garcia, former Senator Gonzalo Barrientos, Richard Moya, John Treviño, Gilbert Martinez, and Joe Morin. Their vision was to create an organization that would serve and represent the business interests of a small but growing Hispanic entrepreneurial class in Austin. To this day, the Chamber's primary goal is to continue the advancement and progression of a strong and stable economic culture for Hispanic businesses. The Chamber strives to reach these goals by developing business, management skills, and bridging access to financial capital while maintaining cultural values and integrity. The GAHCC team is passionate about shaping a Central Texas where Hispanics thrive in business and are impactful leaders in their communities.

A Singular Focus on Success

GAHCC represents a broad array of organizations whose members represent corporations, small businesses, nonprofits, and governmental agencies. Navigated by successful business people and community leaders, the Chamber is a tremendous business resource for entrepreneurs, professionals, or corporations of any size in the Greater Austin area.

A recent study indicated that Hispanic-owned businesses in the area could top 51,000 and contribute over $12.8 billion in revenue to the Central Texas economy by 2020. To serve the business owners generating those phenomenal numbers, the Chamber sponsors a number of initiatives designed to advocate for the Hispanic business community, including: Chamber-sponsored sessions to promote important city issues such as endorsing Austin Bond Propositions A Through G; influencing the effort to bring a Major League Soccer team to Austin; and creating a state legislative agenda.

Ambassador Program Overview GAHCC Ambassadors promote retention by assisting members in maximizing their Chamber membership, welcoming new members, and attending ribbon cuttings and other Chamber events.

Hispanic Austin Leadership The mission of the Hispanic Austin Leadership (HAL) is to provide business leaders and professionals the opportunities to develop business acumen, civic awareness, leadership skills, and a network of colleagues for life.

These and numerous other programs, initiatives, and signature events of the

GAHCC ensure that the organization remains the leading resource and advocate for the Hispanic business community in the Greater Austin area.

Helping African American Business Owners Succeed

The Greater Austin Black Chamber of Commerce (GABC) was incorporated in 1982 with a mission of inspiring, developing, and promoting black economic success in the Greater Austin area. Eleven community, political, and business leaders within Austin came

together with a mission to bring awareness tothe enormous amount of dollars generated from black consumers in the form of travel and tourism within the goal of providing economic prosperity for African American businesses and the general Greater Austin region. The Chamber was designed to serve as a bridge for African American businesses and the Greater Austin business community to obtain increased prosperity and influence within Central Texas.

The GABC has effectively accomplished its mission through the strength of its members. Powered by the collective influence of local businesses and the Chamber's strategic partners, the GABC is uniquely positioned to capture opportunity and advance a business agenda. Member-driven programs, initiatives, and policies create a platform for business connections, professional development, and community involvement.

Guiding Principles

Almost four decades after its founding, the GABC continues its mission of delivering capital to its members, the African American and Greater Austin Business Community through three principle value areas:

- Political Capital: Advocacy and Civic Engagement
- Business Capital: Business Education and Training
- Social Capital: Networking and Business Connections

The Chamber is active in assisting aspiring entrepreneurs in launching a new business venture. Team members provide expertise in areas such as business plan review and development assistance; marketing plan review and development assistance; financial readiness assessment; business management technical assistance; and more.

In addition, a number of signature programs exist to provide meaningful educational and networking opportunities for Chamber members to increase business acumen, access, and visibility. The Chamber hosts a Black Elected Officials program in an effort for residents of the five-county Austin area to network and connect with their government officials.

The State of Black Business program features business experts and leaders as they discuss the state of African American businesses within the Central Texas region.

Evening Networking and Breakfasts provide an opportunity for members and sponsors to network with each other to expand business opportunities.

The Chamber's Taste of Black Austin has become one of the city's most anticipated annual events. The goal of the event is to bring together food, photography, and history of the black food journey and its influence on the larger context of American Culture and business. Food at the event, served as passed small plates and through food stations, reflects stories from black experiences from various times throughout history to present day. At the core of the event is a dynamic group of black chefs who speak to those stories from a curated culinary perspective.

These and other programs, along with member-driven initiatives and a committed Chamber team, have been the cornerstone of the success of the Greater Austin Black Chamber of Commerce.

Advocating. Educating. Empowering.

The Austin LGBT Chamber of Commerce was founded in 1997 with a mission of promoting economic growth in the Austin LGBTQ community through advocacy, connections, and education. The vision of its founders was to help Austin become a fully supportive, diverse, and and prosperous community through a variety of initiatives that would advocate on behalf of businesses whose members represent segments of the community with special concerns or a unifying social mission.

Those programs and initiatives are varied:

- The Chamber's Employee Resource Group (ERG) Roundtable acts as a convener of existing and new ERG groups to provide a forum for education and awareness supporting the professional growth of LGBT individuals by fostering a safe environment within their companies/businesses for individuals to be authentic in the workplace.
- The Advocacy Committee researches ordinances, regulations, and propositions at the local, state, and national levels that will impact the business community.
- The Health & Wellness Committee maps out strategies to convene healthcare providers to impact the health and wellness of LGBT Austin.
- The Business Academy Committee acts as a resource for business members from large to small offering a variety of expert lead panel discussions on best practices in areas such as branding/marketing, business finances, IT/cybersecurity, supplier diversity, and more.
- Young Professionals with Pride is a networking group for the young and young-at-heart whose mission is to empower and strengthen the Young LGBT and allied professional community in Austin through networking, community outreach, and education.

Pride in Achievement

Since its founding, the Austin LBGT Chamber has been recognized for the successful role it has played in promoting the economic growth of the Austin area. In 2015, the organization received the "Excellence in Community Award" from the National Gay and Lesbian Chamber of Commerce. Two years later, the Chamber was awarded CTI Certified designation highlighting the achievements made by the Chamber as a whole.

The Austin LGBT Chamber continues its focus on community. The LGBT Chamber of Commerce Foundation, a nonprofit corporation based in Austin, was founded in 2016 to provide education grants to deserving LGBT residents of the Austin metro area so that they can develop skills and become more successful.

"The Austin LGBT Chamber of Commerce is the oldest of its kind in Texas," states Tina Grider-Cannon, the Chamber's Executive Director. "We are focused on creating a business-friendly environment for our members and the workforce in our region. We do this by advocating, educating, and providing a variety of engagement tools designed to promote economic growth in the Austin LGBTQ and allied community, thereby creating a fully supportive, diverse, and prosperous Austin."

Career Driven. Community Focused.

THE AUSTIN YOUNG CHAMBER PROMOTES THE ECONOMIC INTERESTS OF THE CENTRAL TEXAS BUSINESS COMMUNITY THROUGH PROGRAMS AND INITIATIVES SPECIFICALLY DESIGNED TO BUILD AND STRENGTHEN AUSTIN'S YOUNG PROFESSIONAL WORKFORCE.

Founded in 2009, the Young Chamber is the product of a booming region attracting and retaining a high concentration of young talent. Seeking opportunities where they could learn and grow, founding members came together to form a Chamber unlike any other.

Today the Austin Young Chamber has approximately 550 members and reaches over 10,000 young professionals annually.

"Our Austin Young Chamber membership has contributed significantly to the competitiveness and preparedness of our young professional workforce," stated Heather McKissick, Senior Vice President of Community Impact, University Federal Credit Union. "Through the Young Chamber, employees gain critical leadership skills, experiences, and connections that make our company and our community stronger."

▲ Alyssia Palacios-Woods, President & CEO

DESIGNED FOR SUCCESS

The Young Chamber's vision is for Austin to have the most talented, collaborative, and community focused workforce in the country. Pursuant to that goal, the organization offers a number of programs and initiatives designed to help young professionals succeed:

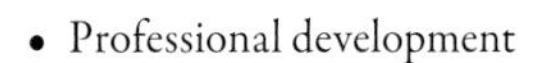

- Professional development
- Civic education and advocacy
- Experiential leadership
- Committee opportunities
- Community engagement
- Business development & networking

In addition, a series of signature events offered annually include the LEAD Summit full-day conference, Casino Social networking event, and FAVE Awards business gala.

Through these efforts, the Young Chamber encourages its target demographic of under 40 to build a dynamic set of skills, experiences, and connections for long-term success. As leaders today, as leaders tomorrow, the Young Chamber takes on the challenge and the opportunity to create a strong future for Austin.

Learn more and become a member at austinyc.org.

Photo by Noah Towery

Greater Austin Asian Chamber of Commerce

A Catalyst for Economic Growth

The 2019 estimated population of Austin is approximately 931,000 people, an increase of more than 124,000 people from the 2010 census. From 2011 to 2016, the fourth largest city in Texas was the fastest growing city in the U.S. with a population growth of almost three percent over those years. The city's Asian Pacific American (APA) community is approximately nine percent of Austin's residents and is growing twice as fast as Austin itself, doubling every 11 years. To better serve this burgeoning population, the Greater Austin Asian Chamber of Commerce (GAACC) was founded with the merger in 2012 of two organizations that had served the APA community for twenty years.

The mission of the GAACC is to promote the APA community and community at large as a catalyst for local and global economic growth through advocacy, connections and education.

The organization serves a very fragmented demographic, including Indian, Chinese, Vietnamese, Korean, and many others, who have very different needs. GAACC provides a bridge to the local APA business community, as well as to markets in Asia.

To be effective in the first role, GAACC builds and maintains strong relationships with the various ethnic Asian groups in order to share information and resources to them, as well as ensure their voice is heard. On the international front, GAACC partners with the City of Austin to plan annual delegations to Asia and acts as a resource for Asian companies looking to locate in Central Texas.

Serving its Members

A recent survey of business owners indicated that in 2019 there were approximately 17,000 APA businesses in the Austin Round Rock Metropolitan Statistical Area. In line with its mission of promoting the APA community, the GAACC offers a number of programs and services designed to be relevant to the various needs and interests of this dynamic demographic and supporting their contributions to the community at large.

Advocacy: The GAACC takes positions on policy issues that impact business as well as the APA community. It helps mainstream organizations understand that they need to disaggregate data for the Asian demographic or provide linguistically and culturally appropriate services to this community since a high percentage are not proficient in English.

Connections: The organization sponsors many events to provide space for people to meet and network with APA businesses. In addition, staff members offer referrals and provide introductions and information to anyone requesting it.

Education: GAACC hosts regular workshops, many of which are free, on a variety of general business and industry specific topics, classes on how to become certified as minority, as well as market briefings on different Asian countries. Bilingual staff are also able to meet with business owners to address specific issues that they may be facing.

The GAACC looks forward to supporting the rising contributions of Austin's APA businesses to the community at large.

Photographer Biographies

Kelly West is a filmmaker and photojournalist who has been documenting local communities for almost two decades. She has won both statewide and nationwide awards for her photo and film work, including a regional Emmy in 2017 for a project documenting the first mass murder in America. Her work has been featured in both local and international publications, including *Texas Monthly*, *The Intercept*, and *Agence France-Presse*. When she's not on assignment, you can find her hanging with her backyard chickens, playing in a ukulele cover band, or canning homemade pickles.

Laura Skelding has spent the last 20 years honing her craft in the demanding, highly dynamic world of Photojournalism. During her 17 years at *The Austin American Statesman*, she was nominated for the Pulitzer Prize and won the admiration of her peers and editors for capturing the character and drama of the world around her. She graduated from the University of Texas at Austin with a bachelor of Photojournalism. She entered the world of Photojournalism in her home town of New Orleans at the *Times Picayune* where she focused on the rich street life and culture of the Big Easy. Currently, she is an in-demand independent commercial photographer who still loves to shoot for editorial clients as well.

You can see more of her work at www.lauraskelding.com

John Langmore left Austin in 1989 after graduating from the University of Texas School of Law for a corporate career. He returned to the city with his family in 2003 and began pursuing photography professionally. He is civically active in Austin on matters related to urban growth. His projects include the books *Fault Lines: Portraits of East Austin* and *Open Range: America's Big-Outfit Cowboy* and the documentary film *Cowboys*, which he codirected and coproduced.

Casey Chapman Ross, an Austin native, graduated from the University of Texas with a Fine Arts Degree in Studio Art and has been a full-time freelance photographer for 6 years. She calls South Austin home with her husband and three children. They enjoy house hunting, camping, Scrabble, watching nature shows and playing outside. When she's not wrangling the kiddos, her work focuses on strengthening the efforts of progressive causes, campaigns, and candidates in Texas and nationwide.

In the summer, 2019 she published *True to Form, a Heartfelt Collection from Beto O'Rourke's 2018 U.S. Senate Campaign*, a compilation of both her work as well as artists' work from around the state and stories from the campaign trail by staff and volunteers. In the Fall 2019, she released *I am an Activist!*, a coloring book educating young readers on the tenants of activism and civic engagement.

"As a champion supporting the efforts she holds dear, Casey is tireless in her efforts to lift up those causes with positive, powerful imagery. Casey is both a historian and a change agent." –Austin City Council Member, Greg Casar

Sean Mathis was adopted in Hawaii by his parents Joan and Stan, and raised in El Paso, Texas, with his older sister, Mary Elizabeth. He swam competitively as a youth, and was sent to the principal's office often for questioning authority and learning the hard way. He took his time in earning his undergraduate degree in RTVF from University of North Texas, and moved to Austin to acquire his Master's in Photojournalism from the University of Texas in 2008, where he was later an adjunct professor.

He currently works for the state of Texas as a media producer, and pursues freelance work whenever possible, with a distinct passion for photographing live music and landscapes. Austin is still his home, though he often travels around the country and the world to capture vivid and profound images and stories. He aspires to improve the world around him, one frame at a time. Sean loves dogs but has only owned felines. He's easily distracted by any chance to snowboard, throw a Frisbee, swim in natural water, and delve into meaningful conversation with friends and strangers, while avoiding small talk at all costs.

IG: @seanson28
sean@seanmathis.com
www.seanmathis.com

Erich Schlegel is an award-winning freelance photographer in Austin, Texas. Erich was born in Monterrey, Mexico to American parents (US & Mexican citizen since birth) and grew up speaking English and Spanish in Mexico, Colombia and Panama. Erich received his BBA in International Business from SMU in Dallas, Texas. However, his passion for photography led him to a career in photojournalism, starting after college at *The Brownsville Herald* on the Texas/Mexico border, then the *Corpus Christi Caller-Times*. Erich then worked at *The Dallas Morning News* from 1988 until 2008. While at the *DMN*, assignments ranged from daily stories to covering multiple Summer and Winter Olympic Games and other major sporting events, long term documentary projects, and conflicts around the world. Erich's specialty, however, was documenting stories in Latin America with emphasis on Mexico and Cuba.

In 2008, Erich left *The Dallas Morning News* to pursue a freelance career. Erich has the ability to shoot still and video images with DSLR cameras above, below, and around water. He also has the capability to shoot remotely with his SLR's and GoPro cameras, including using aerial UAV's. He is a founding partner with Ultralite Films, an award-winning film production team.

Clients include: Getty Images, *National Geographic*, The Nature Conservancy, *Texas Highways Magazine*, *USA Today*, Austin Opera, Grand Trunk Goods and many other publications and companies.

Erich lives near Austin, Texas and is supporting his daughter Thira through her art education at The School of the Art Institute of Chicago. Erich also enjoys fresh and saltwater fishing, surfing, SCUBA diving, marathon canoe racing, skiing and ice climbing.

U.S. citizen. Fluent in Spanish since birth.

(Photographers continued on next page)

Ed Malcik studied photojournalism at the University of Texas and worked as a staff photographer at newspapers, including *The Austin American-Statesman*. He freelanced for the wire services and publications such as *Cosmopolitan*, *Us*, *Texas Monthly*, and *The New York Times*. He served as a Peace Corps Volunteer in The Gambia, and as a Foreign Service Officer at U.S. embassies and consulates around the world. He left diplomacy to return to photography, and now lives in Austin where he photographs on the street in a documentary style. His work has been exhibited in Europe, India, and the United States, and is in the Wittliff Collections. He is represented by Mockingbird Handprints Gallery in San Antonio. More of his work can be seen on Instagram and his web page at EdMalcikPhotography.com. His upcoming book is *The Cat in His Underwear: Photos From Austin.*

Sam Cole began photography at age 7 with 110 camera from a Kellogg's cereal box and has gone on to shoot miles of film and Kodachrome. His work has been featured in the Austin Advocate homeless newspaper as well as spaceweather.com and KXAN Weather News. A resident of Community First! Village, Sam has also shown his photos at the Austin's annual Art from the Streets show.

Noah Towery is an artist and publisher who lives in Memphis, TN. He received an MFA in painting at the Tyler School of Art in Philadephia. You can find his paintings, prints, & photography online. ig: @noahmtown

Selected Bibliography

Books

Burnett, Jonathan. Flash Floods in Texas. College Station, Texas: Texas A&M University Press, 2008.

Busch, Andrew M. City in a Garden: Environmental Transformations and Racial Justice in Twentieth-Century Austin, Texas. Chapel Hill, North Carolina: The University of North Carolina Press, 2017.

Davis, John T. Austin City Limits: 25 Years of American Music. New York, New York: Billboard Books, 2000.

Dell, Michael with Catherine Fredman. Direct from Dell: Strategies that Revolutionized an Industry. New York, New York: HarperCollins, 1999.

Gibson, David V. and Everett M. Rogers. R&D Collaboration on Trial. Boston, Massachusetts: Harvard Business School Press, 1994.

Humphrey, David C. Austin: A History of the Capital City. Austin, Texas: Texas State Historical Association, 1997.

Kerr, Jeffrey Stuart. Seat of Empire: The Embattled Birth of Austin, Texas. Lubbock, Texas: Texas Tech University Press, 2013.

Long, Joshua. Weird City: Sense of Place and Creative Resistance in Austin, Texas. Austin, Texas: University of Texas Press, 2010.

Orum, Anthony M. Power, Money and the People: The Making of Modern Austin. Eugene, Oregon: Resource Publications, 1987.

Patoski, Joe Nick. Austin to ATX: The Hippies, Pickers, Slackers and Geeks who Transformed the Capital of Texas. College Station, Texas: Texas A&M University Press, 2019.

Rothstein, Richard. The Color of Law: A Forgotten History of How Our Government Segregated America. New York, NY: Liveright Publishing Corporation, 2017.

Swearingen, Jr. William Scott. Environmental City: People, Place, Politics and the Meaning of Modern Austin. Austin, Texas: University of Texas Press, 2010.

Tuttle, Thomas C. Growing Jobs: Transforming the Way We Approach Economic Development. Santa Barbara, California: Praeger, 2016.

Wilson, Eddie with Jess Sublett. Armadillo World Headquarters. Austin, Texas: University of Texas Press, 2017.

Wynn, Jonathan. Music City: American Festivals and Placemaking in Austin, Nashville, and Newport. Chicago, Illinois: The University of Chicago Press, 2015.

Articles

Barna, Joel Warren. "The Rise and Fall of Smart Growth in Austin." Cite. Spring 2002. http://www.offcite.org/wp-content/uploads/sites/3/2010/03/TheRiseAndFallOfSmartGrowthInAustin_Barna_Cite53.pdf

Beach, Patrick. "Long a public servant, former Austin mayor Garcia now free to say no." Austin American-Statesman. September 23, 2016. https://www.statesman.com/news/20160923/long-a-public-servant-former-austin-mayor-garcia-now-free-to-say-no

Best of Austin 2003. Austin Chronicle. September 26, 2003. https://www.austinchronicle.com/best-of-austin/year:2003/poll:critics/category:architecture-and-lodging/capital-area-statues-cast-best-commission-of-a-heaving-bosom/

Clark-Madison, Mike. "A Bigger, Better Convention Center." Austin Chronicle. May 24, 2002. https://www.austinchronicle.com/news/2002-05-24/93218/

Corcoran, Michael. "The Thrill Isn't Gone." Texas Monthly. October 2012. https://www.texasmonthly.com/articles/the-thrill-isnt-gone/

Curtin, Kevin. "Gary Clark Jr. on Antones." Austin Chronicle. August 11, 2014. https://www.austinchronicle.com/daily/music/2014-08-11/gary-clark-jr-on-antones/

Dinges, Gary. "Army: Quality of life, tech culture helped Austin land Futures Command." Austin American-Statesman. July 13, 2018 https://www.mystatesman.com/news/local/army-quality-life-tech-culture-helped-austin-land-futures-command/ZGcZQ6lVxkvLpInlDRSUyL/

Bibliography Continued

Fullerton, Kevin. "The Prop. 2 Coup: Not Your Same Old Song and Dance." Austin Chronicle. May 8, 1998. https://www.austinchronicle.com/news/1998-05-08/523434/

Gibson, David V., and John S. Butler. "Sustaining the Technopolis: The Case of Austin, Texas." World Technopolis Review, vol. 2, no. 2, Dec. 2013, pp. 64–80.

Gill, Chris. "Interview: Austin's Gary Clark Jr. Discusses Influences, Gear and His 'Schizophrenic Style." Guitar World. April 9, 2012. https://www.guitarworld.com/gw-archive/interview-austins-gary-clark-jr-discusses-influences-gear-and

Hall, Michael. The City of the Eternal Boom. Texas Monthly. March 2016. https://www.texasmonthly.com/the-culture/austin-and-the-city-of-the-eternal-boom/

Hawkins, Lori. "Austin tech CEO summit will focus on workforce issues, high-tech future." Austin American-Statesman. May 16, 2011. https://www.statesman.com/business/austin-tech-ceo-summit-will-focus-workforce-issues-high-tech-future/Gyjt3RKH2nEso6j49n8MKM/

Ladendorf, Kirk. "Plugged In: 30 years ago, MCC consortium helped 'put Austin on the technology map." Austin American-Statesman. May 25, 2013. https://www.mystatesman.com/business/plugged-years-ago-mcc-consortium-helped-put-austin-the-technology-map/G909TCCNX4p-J15K9yV7RfL/

Long, Joshua. "Constructing the Narrative of the Sustainability Fix: Sustainability, Social Justice and Representation in Austin, TX." Urban Studies, vol. 53, no. 1, 2016, pp. 149–172.

Moritz, Jennifer, Christopher McMahan and Keith R. Phillips. "Austin's High- Tech Industry: Played Out or Just Beginning?" Federal Reserve Bank of Dallas, San Antonio Branch, Issue 1 2006. https://www.dallasfed.org/~/media/documents/research/vista/vista0601.pdf

O'Reilly, Brian. "What's so Great About Admiral Bobby Inman?" Fortune Magazine. November 10, 1986. http://archive.fortune.com/magazines/fortune/fortune_archive/1986/11/10/68258/index.htm

Parker, Mike. "When Liberty Lunch was the Place." Austin American-Statesman. July 30, 2014. https://www.statesman.com/NEWS/20170707/When-Liberty-Lunch-was-the-place

Patoski, Joe Nick. "Willie Nelson — Gonna Catch Tomorrow Now." No Depression: The Journal of Roots Music. August 31, 2004. http://nodepression.com/article/willie-nelson-gonna-catch-tomorrow-now

Patoski, Joe Nick. "Willie Nelson and the Birth of the Austin Music Scene." Texas Almanac 2012-13. Austin Texas: Texas State Historical Association. https://texasalmanac.com/topics/culture/willie-nelson-and-birth-austin-music-scene

Powers, Pike. Building the Austin Technology Cluster: The Role of Government & Community Collaboration in the Human Capital. Federal Reserve Bank of Kansas City. 2004. http://www.kansascityfed.org/PUBLICAT/NewGovernance04/Powers04.pdf

Smilor, Raymond W., David V. Gibson and George Kozmetsky. "Creating the Technopolis: High-Technology Development in Austin, Texas." Journal of Business Venturing, vol. 4, no. 1, 1989, pp. 49–67.

Staff, Jenny. "Turning Point: Relations on the Mend." Austin Chronicle. February 19, 1999. https://www.austinchronicle.com/news/1999-02-19/521207/

Vanscoy, Kayte. "Waller, Waller Everywhere." Austin Chronicle. January 23, 1998. https://www.austinchronicle.com/news/1998-01-23/519447/

Yetman, Canan. "Pygmalion City." Texas Architect. July/August 2016. https://magazine.texasarchitects.org/2016/07/20/pygmalion-city/

Reports

Capital City Innovation. Austin's Innovation District: 2018 Annual Review. Austin, Texas: March, 2019.

Market Street Services. Austin, Texas Business Climate Assessment. Atlanta, Georgia: June 23, 2003.

Market Street Services. Austin, Texas Economic Development Strategy. Atlanta, Georgia: July 30, 2003.

Market Street Services. Greater Austin, Texas Competitive Realities: Opportunity Austin II. Atlanta, Georgia: May 17, 2007.

Market Street Services. Opportunity Austin 4.0: Strategy and Implementation Guidelines. Atlanta, Georgia: September 2017.

Regional/Urban Design Assistance Team Program. Creating a Great Downtown: R/UDAT Review 2000.

Tretter, Eliot. Austin Restricted: Progressivism, Zoning, Private Racial Covenants, and the Making of a Segregated City. Austin, Texas: 2012. https://repositories.lib.utexas.edu/handle/2152/21232

Titan Music Group. The Austin Music Census: A Data-Driven Assessment of Austin's Commercial Music Economy. Austin, Texas: June 2015. http://www.austintexas.gov/sites/default/files/files/Austin_Music_Census_Interactive_PDF_53115.pdf

Workers Defense Project. Building Austin, Building Injustice: Working Conditions in Austin's Construction Industry. Austin, Texas: June 2009. http://www.workersdefense.org/wp-content/uploads/2013/04/Building-_Austn_Report-2.pdf

Online

Dell Medical School. Merck to Locate IT Hub at Dell Med, Helping Fuel Health Innovation: December 14, 2017 https://dellmed.utexas.edu/news/merck-to-locate-it-hub-at-dell-med

Greater Austin Chamber of Commerce. The Samsung Effect. November 30, 2016. https://www.austinchamber.com/blog/the-samsung-effect

Handbook of Texas Online, Mary Jayne Walsh, "BARTON, WILLIAM," accessed September 08, 2018, http://www.tshaonline.org/handbook/online/articles/fba97.

Handbook of Texas Online, Joseph Milton Nance, "REPUBLIC OF TEXAS," accessed September 08, 2018,http://www.tshaonline.org/handbook/online/articles/mzr02.

Handbook of Texas Online, Herbert Gambrell, "LAMAR, MIRABEAU BUONAPARTE," accessed September 08, 2018,http://www.tshaonline.org/handbook/online/articles/fla15.

Time Magazine. The World's 100 Greatest Places of 2018. http://time.com/collection/worlds-greatest-places-2018/

U.S. Army. Press Conference: Army Officials Announce New Army Command. July 13, 2018. https://www.youtube.com/watch?reload=9&v=WL_CsiuTVFU

INDEX

Numerals

A

B

C

D

M

N

O

P

R

S

T

U

V

W

Y

Z

AUSTIN UNLIMITED

is available from the publisher @ www.cityink.com

Other volumes published in the Urban Renaissance Books series include:

Chattanooga's Heroic Drive

Carmel: round about right

Knoxville: Green by Nature

Columbia: city of rivers, vistas, and dreams

Greenville's Grand Design

Nashville: the south's NEW metropolis

Chattanooga: innovation at warp speed

Memphis: 200 years of heart & soul

Knoxville: region on the rise

609 WEST RACQUET CLUB PLACE
MEMPHIS, TN 38117 • 901-483-1001